Speen 25⁰⁰

A Guide to Jewish References
in the Mexican Colonial Era
1521–1821

A Guide to Jewish References in the Mexican Colonial Era 1521–1821

Selected, compiled, and translated by

Seymour B. Liebman

Philadelphia
University of Pennsylvania Press

7405
Printed in the United States of America

CONTENTS

Introduction

While speculations about Mayan descent from the lost ten tribes of Israel have caught the imagination and interest of a number of historians, archaeologists, and anthropologists, little attention has been given to the history of Mexican Jewry during the colonial period, 1521-1821, a particularly regrettable circumstance since the history of Colonial Mexico's Jews does not lack for sources. This little-known story is recorded in the documents of the Inquisition—a history of devotion to faith, of persecution, intrigue, and martyrology, and, not least, of contributions to the national culture of Mexico. Colonial Jewry was a small, but not insignificant, segment of those who peopled Mexico and who, despite the illegality of their presence and the tenuousness of their position, played an important role in its development.

This introduction is not intended to present a panoramic view of the fascinating, exciting, and at times almost fantastic history of the Jews in Mexico. Plots, intrigues, and daring were the basis of their survival. Accounts of systems of communication among prisoners in the secret cells of the Inquisition, the practice of sending one child of a family into a Catholic religious order, the changing of the wording of prayers to throw off suspicion, and feats of courage and bravery outdo fiction in drama and suspense. There were men and women who withstood the turn of the cord and the torture of the *potro* (rack) without revealing the names of their co-religionists, and there were others who implicated literally hundreds of other Jews. Suffice it to say that Colonial Mexico harbored a thriving Jewish colony which constituted an integral part of the territory's life.[1] Jews resided in every part of the country and were represented in every class and at every level. These people deserve honorable notice in the history both of Mexico and of world Jewry.

In the Archivo General de la Nación (hereafter AGN) are 1,553 volumes of Mexican Inquisition Documents, covering the years 1521 to 1823. The Index to these volumes, the *Indice del Ramo de Inquisición*, consists of fifteen volumes of over 3,000 single-spaced typewritten pages. It is arranged neither in chronological order, nor by subject, persons, or in any other fashion accepted by archivists. Fragments of the *proceso*[2] of an individual may be found in three or more different volumes of documents. There are sections as well as whole *procesos* which are either in other Mexican institutions or in other countries. The AGN does not possess all Inquisition documents. (This will be discussed at greater length below and also in Appendix C of this work.) The *Indice* does contain many facts that are not normally found in an index. It is an enumeration of documents as they happened to be picked up by those who made the compilation.[3]

In order to pursue research into the history of Mexican Jewry during the colonial era, it was necessary to prepare a *Guide* of all matters of Jewish interest as they appear in the *Indice*.

From the *Indice* an alphabetical list of names was prepared. This made it possible to locate the various parts of the *proceso* of any individual. A total *proceso* consists of several hearings, some as many as ten or more, held over a period of months and even years.

A knowledge of paleography is indispensable for reading Inquisition documents, but the *Indice* is in modern Spanish. The draft of the *Guide* revealed the vast amount of

[1]Alfonso Toro, *Los Judíos en la Nueva España* (Mexico, Publicaciones del Archivo General de la Nación, 1932), pp. xxii, xxiii.

[2]A glossary has been appended for Spanish terms.

[3]Yolanda Mariel de Ibañez, *La Inquisición en México durante el Sigle XVI* (México, Universidad Nacional Autonoma, 1946), at close of Explicaciones which has unnumbered pages. In future footnotes, the details of publications will be omitted if the author and his book are included in the Bibliography appended hereto.

material available for study. The need to amplify it to include data from other authorative sources was obvious. Research led to the location of more documents, many outside of Mexico. There is no work that lists all Inquisition documents and their location. Even the excellent *Repertorion Bibliográfico,* etc., by A. Millares Carlo is incomplete. There is no record of privately owned documents.

The discovery of additional *procesos* and parts of others began to fill numerous lacunae. Names such as Ana Rodríguez de Matos, Margarita Morera, and Leonor de Caceres appear in accounts of the Inquisition written during the last century, but documents pertaining to them are not in the AGN. Many documents have been hidden or destroyed. For instance, there is a legend that Francisco (Pancho) Villa used many documents that he had seized during the Mexican Revolution to make a victory bonfire in Querétaro or San Luis Potosí.

The data in parentheses are from the following sources: geographical from the *Indice* and other from Luis González Obregón and/or José Toribio Medina. The Appendices include many additional names with explanations.

The Alphabetical List does not, of course, represent a total census of the Jews of Colonial Mexico. The Inquisition was not infallible in its quest for heretics. The List includes only those apprehended or who are named in histories. The latter appear only if there are data in addition to the statement of their faith. It must be noted that even the Inquisition itself did not consistently seek out the Jews. On May 27, 1783, the Mexican Tribunal received an order from the Supreme Council in Spain adivsing it not to imprison Jews or to sequester their property.[4] At the end of the eighteenth century, the work load of the Inquisitors in reading for purposes of censorship the thousands of books arriving in Veracruz and Acapulco and the administration of the Customs House was so great that they requested increases in salary. For more than a century there had been difficulty in filling positions, especially in the provinces. The Inquisitors began to display a greater concern in the growing number of Protestants and the spread of new ideas like those of Voltaire, Locke, and Rousseau, and even the concept of freedom as enunciated in the Bible.[5] The Mexican Inquisition, while normally under the control of the Supreme Council in Spain, often acted autonomously.

Translations herein are not literal and, in a few instances, are quite free. The amanuenses for the Inquisitors were not particular in their spelling, but seem to have been faithful in their reporting. The "criminal" had to read the transcript of his testimony and affirm its correctness. Every turn of the wheel was recorded; every imprecation against the Inquisitors or the Church was noted; every groan was immortalized. Instead of the designations *marranos* or *cryptojudíos,* the *Santo Oficio's* terms, e.g., *"judío"* or *"judaizante,"* etc., have been used. In the Appendices, the terms follow those of the authors cited.

There is little difference between "b" and "v" in Spanish, and these letters appear interchangeably in the names in the *Indice.* The letters "x," "j," and "s" can be sounded almost alike. The name Juárez is found to begin with any of these letters and may apply to the same person.[6] Many writers were not aware that Rios was used as an abbreviation for Rodríguez by many amanuenses.[7] Undoubtedly, some errors have been made as a result of this confusion, in addition to those which are the author's. For the latter, apologies are extended. Archival material in Spain and documents in Amsterdam

---

[4] José Toribio Medina, *Historia del Tribunal del Santo Oficio de la Inquisición en México,* p. 306.

[5] Luis González Obregón, *México Viejo,* p. 718.

[6] In 1946, Prof. J. Horace Nunemaker wrote that "punctuation, capitalization and accentuation are wholly erratic and utterly inconsistent in the documents," "Inquisition Papers of Mexico," *Research Studies of State College of Washington,* Vol. XIV (March, 1946), No. 1, p. 4.

[7] Obregón, *op. cit.,* p. 681. David Fergusson in his translation of the "Trial of de Granada," *PAJHS,* VII, p. 33, has two footnotes concerning the sisters Catalina de Silva, alias Enriquez and Rafaela Enriquez. For the former, he names the father Antonio Rios Arias and for the latter Antonio Rodríguez Arias. They were the same person.

and other places are not included. Some other places where documents or information may be found are listed in the Bibliography and Appendices.

In the Alphabetical List at the back of this book, there appears the family name followed by a comma, and then the given name, dash, and mother's maiden name. This is not the usual form. It was chosen because it adapted itself more readily to this list and because maternal maiden names were not always used nor were they always correctly given.

The Bibliography is selective. There is great need for a critical analysis of much of the bibliography in the field. Even the best of scholars have erred. The renowned Henry C. Lea in his *History of the Inquisition in the Spanish Dependencies*, p. 208, confused Luis de Carvajal, the governor, with the nephew of the same name. This error no doubt stems from the reliance placed by Mr. Lea on Vicente Riva Palacio's *El Libro Rojo* (Vol. I, 2d ed., México 1905, p. 265). Other authors, e.g., Pablo Martínez del Rio and Yolanda Mariel de Ibañez, have commented on the errors in earlier histories.

In addition to errors, there are ignoble characterizations and aspersions on many of the customs and prayers of the Jews. Some Christian authors of note, to whom these aspects of Jewish life were meaningless or unintelligible, found "witchcraft and magic" or mimicry of the Holy Communion in devout prayers and mores which antedate Christianity.[8]

Without going too far afield, certain comments and hypotheses will be advanced and some questions posed. This liberty is being taken because of the many ramifications and facets of Mexican Jewish history which have not yet been recorded in any language and which, it is hoped, will inspire scholars and those seeking subjects for doctoral dissertations to make further explorations in this field.

The history of the Jews in Mexico commences with the conquest by Cortes in 1521. There were Jews in his company. One of them, Hernando Alonso, has the distinction of being the first Jew burned at the stake on the North American continent. This took place in Mexico City in 1528. From 1502 to 1802 decrees were issued by the Spanish Crown and the Papal authorities prohibiting the entry of Moors or Jews into the New World. Many of these decrees specifically barred them or their descendants from Mexico. To be licensed to enter Nueva España, one had to prove Christian ancestry for the previous four generations. Intrigue and subterfuge helped to circumvent the decrees.

Though *El Tribunal del Santo Oficio* (The Court of the Holy Office) was not officially inaugurated in Mexico until 1571, Franciscans, Dominicans, and bishops under their episcopal powers had already been exercising inquisitorial functions, including *autos de fe*, since 1523. Its dominion included all of Mexico and Central America, except Panama, and the Philippine Islands.

The Jews came initially from Portugal and Spain, but in the seventeenth century they came as nationals from other countries as well. They came with forged passports and through bribes to captains of ships. Their names were not readily identifiable as Jewish and many did not use their father's family name. Undoubtedly, many names were taken from tombstones. There was not a wide range in the use of names. Many in the same family bore identical given names. Other brothers bore different family names. Rodríguez was the most common family name, comprising almost 10 per cent of the total in the appended Alphabetical List. The family relationship was not as great as may be surmised, although many did come from the same towns in Spain and Portugal.

In the midst of the general community, the Jews maintained their own religious life, with functionaries to minister to their needs from the cradle to the grave. There were local leaders and teachers in addition to those who came from abroad to raise money for other Jewish communities. These fund raisers were learned and, to collect the *farda* (aid for overseas brethren), they had to study with and teach their hosts. Mexican Jews remained loyal to their faith in spite of all dangers. They were Jews by choice.

[8]Genaro García, *Documentos ineditos o muy raros de la Historia Mexicana*, Vol. XXVIII, p. 244; and Julio Jiménez Rueda, *Herejias y Superstitiones*, pp. 89-138.

Many died for their faith when they could have recanted and continued to live.

They were devoted to the Old Testament, the Apocrypha and, not surprisingly, especially to the Book of Esther. Queen Esther's failure to reveal her religion until the moment of danger was a reflection of their own *modus vivendi*, and Haman symbolized the omnipresent danger of the Inquisition. Indubitably, study will reveal many Sephardic Jewish customs which no longer exist. The community reflected the life about them. Their personal lives ran the gamut from courtesan and slave trader to those who have been termed saintly.

"In 1618, and in the years following, they [the Jews] went from Brazil to Buenos Aires and thence to Peru, Paraguay and Chile."[9] There were, the *Indice* reveals, many who emigrated from Peru to Mexico, and it is known that Mexican Jews traveled to various parts of the West Indies and the northern parts of Spanish America. Where did those Jews flee who escaped the clutches of the Inquisition, before and after apprehension, from 1642 to 1660? Little credence is to be placed in theories that they sought seclusion among the Indians, and it would be useful to investigate the coincidence in time between the flight of many Jews from Mexico, circa 1649, and the founding of new Jewish settlements in the West Indies, such as the one in Barbados in 1654.[10]

Some historians have intimated that the Inquisition's efforts from 1642 to 1659 to exterminate all vestiges of Jewry in Mexico were successful. The *Indice* reveals a decrease in the number of *procesos* against Jews after 1659. Jews, however, do appear as late as 1795, and on September 16, 1802, another Edict by the Inquisitor General was issued against the entry of Jews into Mexico.[11] Such edicts were never issued unless groups of Jews in Mexico had been found whose presence the Inquisition desired to declare illegal.

The experience of Mexican Jewry is a part of world Jewish history, since the Jews of Mexico were not isolated from other Jewish communities. Just as Simón Vaez Sevilla, in the seventeenth century, had ships trading in all parts of the civilized world, individual Jews were traveling from Mexico to all parts of Europe, Africa, the Near East, the Philippines, and Japan.

An etymological study should be made of several words, among which are *judaizante, dogmatista, jugadora, judío, rabino, rabina,* and *verdugo.*

The desire of the Jews to remain in Mexico when escape was possible poses another question. Could it be that, having been born in Mexico, or having lived there for many years, they came to regard the country as their native land to the extent that, despite insecurity and travail, they preferred to remain than to flee? An example of this attitude is supplied by an excerpt from Fritz Baer's "Die Juden in Christlichen Spanien."[12] Francisco Caceres, a Jew, returned to his native Spain which he had left as a result of the 1492 Decree of Expulsion. He was caught by the Inquisition and his explanation was, "If the King should order the Christians to become Jews or else to leave his realms, some would become Jews and others would leave; and those who left, as soon as they saw their sad plight, would become Jews so they could return to their native place, and be Christians and pray like Christians and deceive the world; they would be Christians."

In an article, "Inquisition Papers of Mexico,"[13] J. Horace Nunemaker wrote:

> *If for no other reason, because of the wealth of local and other historical detail, these documents are of inestimable value for the history of America, and, in particular, for the history of Mexico. Because the Inquisition left no stone unturned in tracking down in minutest detail, not only the genealogy, but the entire personal experience of their prisoners, their investigation brought forth and preserved in their official documentary records the life of the people of their time. We are able to know what they ate and drank, the living conditions in their homes, their work and their travel, their joys and sorrows not to mention their*

[9]A. Wiznitzer, *Jews in Colonial Brazil* (New York, Columbia University Press, 1960), p. 41.
[10]S. M. Shilstone, *Jewish Monumental Inscriptions in Barbados* (Philadelphia, 1957).
[11]AGN, Vol. 1408, pp. 2-3.
[12]Américo Castro, *The Structure of Spanish History,* p. 467.
[13]J. Horace Nunemaker, *op. cit.,* p. 3.

religious life and practice, which were, of course, at variance with the Church and often in active conflict with it.

The words of Professor Nunemaker have even greater application to the sources for a study of the history of the Jews in Mexico during the colonial era.

This Guide is but the skeleton on which there must be placed the flesh and bones of the people who had the indomitable will to live as Jews.

Index to the *Indice del Ramo*

References of Jewish Interest in the 15-volume Index to Inquisition
Documents in the Mexican National Archives

Abbreviations

a of Jewish interest
a/k/a—Also known as
b.—Born
C.C.-Criminal case
D.—Don
Da.—Doña
Dec.—Declaration
Dec'd—Deceased
Den.—Denunciation
Inf.—Information
Inq.—Inquisition
p or pp—Pages in Document Volume but,
    for example, 15pp indicates the
    length of the document while
    p15 indicates by page number
    the location in the Vol.
Pen.—One who was punished by the Inq.
Port.—Portugal or Portuguese
Pro.—Proceso

r.—Resident or reside
Rec.—Reconciled
Rel.est.—Relajado en estatua (burned in
    effigy)
Rios.—Rodríguez
S.O.—Holy Office of the Inq.
Test.—Testimony
To.—Index Volume (Tomo)
Vol.—Volume of Documents

Key to Charges

(1) por judío
(2) por judaizante
(3) por suspechoso judío
(4) por sospechoso judaizante or
    judaismo
(5) child of reconciled
(6) relapsed or second offender
(7) observer of the Law of Moses
(8) ser judío (to be a Jew)

Where there are two family names, the first is that of the bearer and the second is his or her mother's family name.

Document No. Column—if no name precedes the No., the place is Mexico City.

Places in italics are towns in Mexico.

An Alphabetical List and Glossary are appended.

Tomo 1 and 1A consists of 218 pages and covers Volumes 1 to 280 inclusive of Documents.

No.	Year	Vol.	Pages	Document No.	Name of Accused or Document	Charge and Comments
1	1523	1		2	First edict against heretics and Jews	
2	1539	1A	15pp	10	Anton Carmona	(1) Pro. & dec. by sister-in-law
3	1539	1A	1p	18	García Hernández	(1) Pro.
4	1539	1A	24pp	19	Beatriz Hernández	(1) Pro.
5	1539	1A	25pp	20	Rodrigo de Soria	(1) Dec.
6	1539	1A	24pp	21	Francisco Serrano	(1) Dec.
7	1539	1A	p28	22	Juan Ruiz	(1) Dec., b. Jerez de la Frontera, Castile
8	1544	1A		25	a Memo of children of those burned at stake or rec. who were in Mexico	

No.	Year	Vol.	Pages	Document No.	Name of Accused or Document	Charge and Comments
9	1536	2	131pp	2	González Gómez (correct first name is Gonzálo)	(2) Pro., r. *Michoacán*
10	1537-1539	22	1p	9	Manuel Borullo (Port.)	(3) Pro.
11	1537-1539	22	1p	9	Juan Ruiz (Port.)	(3) Pro.
12	1537	22	1p	9	Diego Machuca	(3) Pro., b. Duero
13	1538	30	1p	5	Pedro Hernández de Alvor	(8) Pro., b. Villa de Playa, Azores
14	1538	30	63pp	8	Francisco Millan, tavernkeeper	(4) Pro., b. Utrera, Port. Special Judge for torture
15	1539	30	114pp	9A	Alvaro Mateos, acquitted	(2) Pro., b. Medillin, son of new Christians
16	1539	30	67pp	9A	Beatriz Gómez, acquitted	(2) Pro., wife of Alvaro Mateos
17	1554	30		*Zumpango* 13	Hernández de Cazalla	(4) Inf. filed by Vicar of *Mines* of *Zumpango*
18	1564	31	8pp	14 a	Diego Díaz	Inf., son of Moxito burned at the stake in Llerena
19	1539	40	1p	3d	Juan Cercado	Dec., suspicion of being a Jewish convert in Ocaña, Spain
20	1539	40	1p	3e	Antonio de Heredia	Dec., same as 19 *supra*, b. Toledo
			1p	3f	García de Moron	b. Seville
21	1570	44	13pp	*Durango* 1	Martín Arana	(4) Pro. and failure to attend mass
22	1571	49	14pp	5	Leonor Arias	(3) Pro., r. *Compostela*
23	1571	49	6pp	8	Juan Ortiz	(3) Pro., balance Vol. 51, p. 17
24	1572	52	15pp	*Nicaragua* 2	Diego Andrada Pardo	(1) Pro.
25	1574	58	11pp	*Tuxtla* 1	Jorge Hernández	(3) Pro., Port. mariner
26	1575	59	235pp	*Tula* 1	Fernándo Alvarez Pliego	(1) Pro., Port.
27	1576	59	27pp	*Tlaxcala*	Juan Ruiz Ortiz	(3) Pro., commercial agent
28	1579	59	146pp	6	García González Bermegero	(2) Pro. (rel. in person)

No.	Year	Vol.	Pages	Document No.	Name of Accused or Document	Charge and Comments
29	1579	59		7	Gonzálo de León, goldsmith Francisco Rosado Nuño Ruiz	Grandchildren of relaxed persons
30	1575	66		*Mérida Yuc.* 4	Cristobal de Miranda	Inf. Dean of Cathedral of Yucatán, descendant of relapsed
31	1571	71	16pp	37	<u>a</u> (Report of visit made to secret prison of Inq. by Pedro Moya de Contreras, first official Inquisitor of S. O. in Mex.)	
32	1572	75	6pp	*Mérida* 3	Cristobal de Miranda	Letter to S. O.
33	1574-1632	77	63pp	35	(Acts and efforts made to learn about old and recent sambenitos and position of those remitted by the S. O.)	
34	1575	79	2pp	*Mérida* 10	Cristobal de Miranda	Den. by Pedro Salinas
35	1575	80	6pp	8	Cristobal de Miranda	Dec. of Juan González Noguera *et al*
36	1575	80	41pp	17	Cristobal de Miranda	Letters of Miranda to S. O. and of Comisario of S. O.
37	1576	81	34pp	*Tlaxcala* 17	Pedro Núñez de Montalvan	Pro. for being son of one relaxed
38	1577	82	2pp	*Yucatán* 34	Cristobal de Miranda	Letters of Bishop Diego de Landa re Miranda's lineage
39	1577	82	22pp	35	Diego Herrador, shoemaker	Pro., grandson of one burned at stake
40	1577	83	20pp	*Yucatán* 4	Cristobal de Miranda	12 letters in his defense and letter of Comisario against Bishop Diego de Landa's persecution
41	1578	84	36pp	22	Cristobal de Miranda	17 letters
42	1530	89	14pp	36	<u>a</u> Inf. against children of those remitted or were burned at the stake and who were illegally in New Spain	
43	1581	90	47pp	*Veracruz* 38	Beatriz González, wife of Francisco Rodríguez, barber; Isabel de Ocampo, wife of Bernabe Gierra, swordcutter; and other sisters and daughters of Juan González, dec'd	Pro.; Juan González was condemned by Inq. at Llerena, which sent letter with total lineage to S. O. of *Mexico*

No.	Year	Vol.	Pages	Document No.	Name of Accused or Document	Charge and Comments
44	1539	125	3pp	1	Juan de Salamanca, barber	(3) Pro.
45	1540	125	41pp 20pp	5 7	Juan de Baeza Juan de Baeza	(3) Pro.; he circumcised some children and one was an Indian child. In the second hearing, the Judge was the same but there was a different Fiscal
46	1581	125	1p	25	Baltazar Rodríguez	Dec. for being son of Blanca Lorenzo (5)
47	1582	125	2pp	54	Fray Lorenzo Altamirano or Fray Angel	Den. by monk for being (5) and brother of Jews burned at stake at Llerena
48	1584	126	8pp	5	Pedro Ponce de León Ayala	Pro., son of D. Juan Ponce de León relaxed in person by Inq. at Seville
49	1585	126	7pp	*Michoa-clán* 6	Fray Luis Mener	(3) Pro., Franciscan monk, Guardian of convent at *Aguacatlán*
50	1589	126	47pp	11	Gonzálo Pérez Ferro (Port.) (tortured, rec. 1601)	(2) Pro., son of Gonzálo Pérez Ferro
51	1589	126	131pp	12	Fray Gaspar de Carbajal, Isabel Rodríguez Andrada, Luis de Carabajal, Gov. of Reyno de León, Luis de Carvajal, mozo	(2) Pro., Dominican monk (see also the Riva Palacio Collection). This Pro. has information about the families who were penanced: Duarte, Carvajal, Rodríguez, Núñez, Almeida, and declarations against the individuals in adjoining column.*
52	1589	126	129pp	13	Doña Mariana Núñez	(2) Pro., daughter of Francisco Rodríguez Matos & Francisca Carvajal
53	1589-1592	127	207pp	1	Tomas de Fonseca Castellanos	(3) Pro., 2 cases, b. Visseo, Port.
54	1589	127	123pp	2	Hernándo Rodríguez de Herrera	(2) Pro., b. Cubillana

*A compilation of the Index to the Riva Palacio Collection will be appended to this compilation.

No.	Year	Vol.	Pages	Document No.	Name of Accused or Document	Charge and Comments
55	1589	127	58pp	3	Lic. Manuel de Morales	(2) Pro., Port., doctor. He was a Jew in Venice
56	1582	133		26	a 2 edicts by S. O. re Notaries, Jews and Lutherans	
57	1596	149	96pp	2	Hernándo Rodríguez de Herrero	(2) Pro., b. Fondón, Port.
58	1590	150	56pp	1	Jorge de Almeyda*	(3) Pro., Port. miner in *Taxco*
59	1593	150	13pp	*Puebla* 6	Pedro de la Rozaval	(3) Inf.
60	1594	151	172pp	*Tlaxcala* 3	Daniel Benitez, tailor	(1) Pro., b. Borgoñon, r. in *Tacamachalco*
61	1594	151	248pp	6	Manuel Gómez Navarro (Port.)	(2) Pro., b. San Martin de Trevejos; son of Jorge Núñez and Juana Gómez
62	1594	152	116pp	*Guadala-jara* 1	Diego Flores	(3) Pro., encomendero, *Xuchipilia*
63	1594	152	110pp	2	Ana Vaez, wife Jorge Alvarez	(2) Pro., b. Fondón, Port.
64	1595	152	66pp	3	Francisco Vaez (b. San Vicente Davera, Port.)	(2) Pro., servant of Manuel de Lucena of *Pachuca*
65	1595	152	299pp	4	Catalina Enrique, wife of Manuel Lucena	(2) Pro., r. *Pachuca*
66	1595	153	194pp	1	Jorge Alvarez (rec. 1601)	(2) Pro., Port.
67	1595	153	11pp	2	Gabriel Enríquez	(2) Pro., Port., bachelor
68	1595	153	115pp	7	Clara Enriquez (widow of Fran- cisco Méndez)	(2) Pro., Port.
69	1595	153	24pp	8	Blanca de Morales, wife of Pedro Her- nández (rel. est. 1601)	(2) Pro., sister of Lic. Manuel de Morales
70	1595	153	156pp	9	Beatriz Enríquez la Payba widow of Simon Ros. Payba	(2) Pro., b. Fondón, Port.
71	1595	153			Simon Rodríguez	Pro., merchant. See Criminal Branch, vol. 685
72	1595	153	30pp	10	Juan Rodríguez de Silva	(2) Pro.

*González Obregón (hereafter L.G.O.) p. 685; relaxed in person, 1596; González Obregón p. 691; rel. est. 1609; fugitive.

No.	Year	Vol.	Pages	Document No.	Name of Accused or Document	Charge and Comments
73	1595	154	236pp	1	Justa Méndez, maiden	(2) Pro., daughter of Clara Enríquez
74	1595	154	121pp	2	Costanza Rodríguez, wife of Sebastian Rodríguez	(2) Pro., Port.
75	1595	154	25pp	3	Isabel Clara, wife of Franco Hernández, brother of Lic. Manuel de Morales	(1) Pro., Port. (fugitive; rel. est. 1601)
76	1595	154	129pp	4	Pedro Enríquez, bachelor	(1) Pro., son of Simon Payba
77	1595	155	76pp	1	Andre Rodríguez	(1) Pro., b. Fondón, Port.
78	1595	155	138pp	2	Ana López, wife of Diego López Regalon	(2) Pro., r. *Castelo Blanco* (but L.G.O., p. 683, states b. Fondon & r. Mex. City)
79	1595	155	109pp	3	Leonor Diaz, wife of Francisco Rodríguez Desa (rec. 1596)	(2) Pro., b. Seville
80	1595	155	148pp	4	Sebastian de la Peña, bachelor (Port.)	(2) Pro., b. San Juan de Pesquera
81	1595	156	80pp	1	Manuel Rodríguez	(2) Pro., b. Fondón, Port.
82	1595	156	72pp	2	Jorge Vaez (Port.)	(2) Pro., b. San Vicente Davera, Port.
83	1595	156	86pp	3	Francisco Rios, alias Francisco Núñez, husband of Justa Méndez	(2) Pro., b. San Vicente Davera, Port.
84	1595	156	287pp	4	Tomas de Fonseca Castellanos	(6) Second trial, r. *Taxco*
85	1596	157	240pp	1	Ruy Diaz Nieto (rec. 1601)	(2) Pro., b. Oporto, Port.
86	1596	157	31pp	2	Juan Rodríguez, soapmaker	(2) Pro., Port., rel. est.
87	1596	157	104pp	3	Duarte Rodríguez (Port.)	(2) Pro., b. Cubellano, Port.
88	1596	157	2pp	Chiapa 3A	Juan Martinez de la Torre	(3) Inf.
89	1596	157	27pp	5	Francisco Rodríguez	(2) Pro., b. San Vicente Davera, Port.
90	1596	158	126pp	1	Hector de Fonseca, miner	(2) Pro., b. Visseo, Port.; r. *Taxco* (rec. 1601)
91	1596	158	26pp	2	Miguel Hernández (r. *Taxco;* fugitive; rel. est. 1601)	(2) Pro., b. Visseo, Port.

No.	Year	Vol.	Pages	Document No.	Name of Accused or Document	Charge and Comments
92	1596	158	133pp	3	Tomas de Fonseca (note similarity name 84), Port.	(2) Pro., b. Freyja de Espadacinto; r. *Tlalpuxahua*
93	1596	158	141pp	4	Antonio Diaz Marquez, merchant	(2) Pro., b. Alvala, near Lisbon
94	1596	159	293pp	1	Antonio Díaz de Cáceres	(2) Pro., Port.
95	1596	159	61pp	2	Diego Diez Nieto, bachelor	(2) Pro., b. Oporto, Port.
96	1596	159	22pp	3	Andres Núñez (2 Edicts with Great Seal)	(2) Pro., b. Mogodorio, Port.
97	1596	159	32pp	4	Antonio de Fonseca	(2) Accusation made by Diego Nieto (note name 95)
98	1597	159	96pp	5	Manuel Alvarez, merchant; b. Fondón, Port.	(2) Certification (rec. 1601)
99	1597	160	141pp	Manila 1	Manuel Gil de la Guardia	(2) Port., a new Christian
100		160			Francisco Rodríguez, silversmith	(2) Pro., Port.
101	1597	160	13pp	2	Antonio Fernández and his wife Antonio Gómez, innkeeper (b. Villa Nueva de Poliman; Alberguez). Jorge Fernández Jorge Rodríguez (b. Seville; ass't. at Mines of *Pachuca;* rec. 1601) Duarte Rodríguez Simon Rodríguez (rec. 1601)	(2) Test. of Ana de Sosa
102	1957	160	30pp	11	Francisco Rodríguez, alias Francisco Rodríguez de Cea	(2) Pro., 2 Edicts with Great Seal (rel. est. 1596)
103	1597	160	101pp	12	Diego López Regalon, dec'd, alias Felipe López (b. Fondón, Port.; merchant; rel. est. 1601)	(2) Pro., against his memory. Former prisoner at Los Reyes, Peru
104	1597	160	188pp	13	Antonio Gómez	(2) Pro., Port., tortured
105	1597	160	27pp	14	Alvaro González (b. Fondón; rel. est. 1601)	(2) Pro., Port., absent (6)
106	1597	161	28pp	1	Alvaro Rodríguez Achocado	(2) Pro., Port. (rel. est. 1601)

No.	Year	Vol.	Pages	Document No.	Name of Accused or Document	Charge and Comments
107	1597	161	28pp		Luis Díaz (Port., fugitive)	(2) Pro., silversmith (rel. est. 1601)
108	1597	162	Entire Vol.		Diego Hernández Victoria	(2) Pro., b. Oporto, Port.
109	1597	163	187pp	Manila 1	Diego Hernández Victoria	Continuation of 108
110	1597	163	246pp	3	Manuel Javares	(2) Pro., b. Cubellano, Port.
111	1598	164	99pp	3	Bernardo de Luna (check Vol. 112, p112, for same name, accused of eating kid during Lent)	(2) Pro., b. Lisbon, Port.
112	1598	164	103pp	7	Jorge Fernández (rec. 1601)	(2) Pro., b. Salceda, Port.
113	1560	166		3A	a Report of public autos in Seville of Sept. 24, 1559; Dec. 22, 1560; April 26, 1562; Oct. 23, 1562; Oct. 30, 1563; May 13, 1566	
114	1598	167	27pp	3	Sebastian de la Peña	(7) Pro., previously rec.
115	1599	168	19pp	1	Antonio de Morales	Pro., nephew of Lic. Manuel de Morales
116	1523	179	8pp	3	Marcos Rodríguez and Simona de Lucerna, his wife	(2) Pro. [Date obviously wrong, as it should be 1640]
117	1596	209	6pp	Habana 1	Juan Méndez, candy mfr.	(2) Pro., Port. (only fragment)
118	1598	210	258pp	2	Juan Núñez de Leon, official of the Royal Mint	(4) Pro., also accused of *alumbrado*
119	1590	213	7pp	16	a Report of the cases of the public auto de fe in Mexico, Feb. 24, 1590, in La Iglesia Mayor (the Cathedral)	
120	1592	213		44	a More of the autos of 1590 and Dec. 3, 1592	
121	1594	215	16pp	*Guatemala* 2	Fray Lorenzo Altamirano	Pro., b. Alburquerque, in Estremadura, son of Gracía Rol and Lorenzo Angel, condemned for being a Jew in Llerena
122	1595	216	23pp	10	Inf. and Den. against Jews absent on St. Peter's Day	
123	1596	216	43pp	20	a Publication of public auto de fe celebrated in Great Plaza	
124	1597	217	34pp	*Tlaxcala* 6	Martinez de Briones *(Puebla)*	Pro., he called an official of the S. O. "Jew dog"

No.	Year	Vol.	Pages	Document No.	Name of Accused or Document	Charge and Comments
125	1614	220	4pp		Juan Martin de Alexandre of *Zamora, Michoacán*	(2) Inf. (improperly filed with Magdalena Isabel, pp 24-28)
126	1623	220	4pp	3	Jorge Rodríguez, alias Jorge Ruiz	(2) Pro. C. C.
127	1625	221	50pp	2	Pedro de Silva Sauceedo (Port.)	(2) Pro., C. C., r. *Guatemala*
128	1576	223	p48	18	a 5 letters from Inq. at Madrid giving names of descendants of those remitted and penanced	
129	1576	223	p54	19	Pedro de San Lucas Luisa de Abrego	(4) Also Inf. of auto of Feb. 19, 1576
130	1595	223	p158 p170		Letter from Inq. at Madrid about Jews, part of the fleet that burned in Cadiz in 1596 (?) and also of *Simon Rodriguez*	
131	1593	223	p222 ⋮ p225	31	Hernándo Rodríguez de Herrera (rec.) Francisco Núñez (rec.) Francisco Carbajal (rec.) Catalina de León (rec., 1590)	Draft of a letter from S. O. to Inquisitor General, *et al*
132	1593	223	p246 p246 p249 p249 p249 p249	32	Rodríguez Alvaro Simon Rodríguez Felipa López María Gómez Navarro P. Enriquez Pedro Rodríguez	(2) Draft of letter to (2) various other Inqisi- (2) tors for data on the (2) list of accuseds (2) (2)
133	1599	223	p263 p263 p263 p268 p268 p269 p270 p275 p276 p282 p280 p284	33	Duarte Rodríguez Manuel Gil de la Guardia; Rodrigo de Campo (public scribe); Manuel Gil María de Lucena Beatriz de Morales or de Rivera Francisco López Enriquez Luis Díaz Hernándo Alonso and Alonso Guerra Luis Díaz Francisco López Enriquez	(2) [Same comment as (2) 132] (Port.) (r. (2) Manila, rec. 1601) (2) (b. Villa de Quin- (2) tanar) (2) (2) (2) (2) (2) (2) (2)
134	1606-1611	223	p299 p303 p305 p306	34	Diego Hernández Victoria Francisco López Enriquez Andres Núñez Luis Díaz	(2) [Same comment as for 132]

No.	Year	Vol.	Pages	Document No.	Name of Accused or Document	Charge and Comments
135	1611-1616	223	p355 p355 p355 p384	35	Luis Díaz Diego López Isabel de Lucena Gonzalo Molino, scribe of *Taxco* Alonso Ramirez	(2) Correspondence (2) from S. O. of Mexico (2) to various other Inquisitors (grandson of Antonio Machado, rec.)
136	1594	223	p409 p427 p436 pp450,455 p457 p457 p458 p461 p466 p471 p471 p471 p480		Francisco Jorge, Taxco (rel. est. 1596) Francisco Vaez Jorge Vaez Juan Méndez Manuel Cardoso Cristobal Gómez (fugitive) Antonio Núñez Miguel Ruiz Jorge Vaez Francisco Vaez Francisco Rodríguez Francisco Fernández Manuel Tovares (b. Cubillana)	(2) Letters to other (2) Inquisitors (2) (2) (2) (2) Rel. est. 1601 (2) (2) (2) (2) (2) b. San Vicente, rel. est. 1601 (2) (2) Port.
137	1598	223	p492 p496 p499		Diego Hernández Victoria Francisco Navarro Manuel Hernández Diego Gómez Antonio Núñez	(2) Letters to other Inquisitors for (2) information (2) (2) (2)
138	1572-1599	224-237			These volumes contain testimony against various people but neither names or crimes are listed in index	
139	1597	238	p144	13	Manuel de Acosta	(3) Pro., complete, 23 leaves
140	1591-1594 1598	239 248			These volumes (239 to 248) also contain testimony and declarations according to a list in the Vol. of which many concern Jews but neither the Documents nor names are listed in the Index Tomos. Vol. 245 covers 1599	
141	1599	249	p113	13	Isabel de Sosa	(3) Pro.
142	1598	251	136pp	Manila 1	Diego Hernández Victoria	Sequestration of property by S. O.
143	1599	251	98pp	Manila 2	Diego Hernández Victoria	Demand by a 3d person for his property
144	1592	251A		3	a Contains a model of a sambenito de paño	
145	1594 1607	251A 463pp 254A p506		5	Jorge de Almeida	Pro. to secure dowry from Leonor de Andrada Sequestration of property

No.	Year	Vol.	Pages	Document No.	Name of Accused or Document	Charge and Comments
146	1595	252A	28pp	1	Andres Rodríguez (of *Texcoco*)	Sequestration of property
147	1597	252A	5pp	2	Ana López, widow of Diego López	Sequestration of property
148	1595	252A	4pp	1A	Manuel Tavares	Sequestration of property
149	1597	252A	8pp	2A	Jorge Alvarez (rec.)	Sequestration of property
150	1597	252A	13pp	2C	Leonor Rodríguez, wife of Manuel Alvarez (Port.)	Sequestration and auction of her husband's and Jorge Alvarez property
151	1598	252A	102pp	4	Juan Antonio Doria	Sequestration of property
152	1598	252A	2pp	5A	Juan Flamenco	Sequestration of property
153	1598	252A	7pp	5B	Martin Diaz	Sequestration of property
154	1599	252A	54pp	6	Cristobal Miguel	Sequestration of property
155	1600	254	Entire Vol.	a	Book and resumé of all procesos, affairs, and instructions about various people in the secret jails of the Inquisition	
156	1601	254A	4pp	4A	Francisco Rodríguez (Port.), shoemaker	Sequestration of goods (b. Estarcertain)
157	1601	254A	4pp	4B	Francisco Rodríguez	Penitent, auction of his property
158	1601	254A	13pp	4C	Ana Baez, wife of Jorge Alvarez Francisco López Enriquez	Secured a 2d judgment against López property
159	1601	254A	3pp	4D	Antionio Gómez (Port.)	Sale of his goods (Rec. 1605)
160	1601	254A	7pp	4E	Rodrigo Tavares of Villa de la Purificación	Sequestration of possessions
161	1601	254A	19pp	10	Simon de Santiago	Sale of property, relapsed
					Jorge Fernández	Sale of property, relapsed
					Jorge Alvarez	Sale of property, relapsed
162	1604	254A	p506	9	Antonio Méndez (Port.)	Wearing silk clothing, rec.
163	1602	256	1p	7E	Manuel Tavares (rec. 1601)	Den. not wearing his sambenito

No.	Year	Vol.	Pages	Document No.	Name of Accused or Document	Charge and Comments
164	1601	256	4pp	10	Francisco de Caudía	(4) Accusation
165	1602	256	3pp	11	Antonio Rodríguez Carrasco	(2) Den. by Clara de Rivera, herself tried for same crime
166	1601	256	5pp	15N	Andres Ferreira, *clerigo* Anton Rodríguez Diego Hernández Sebastian Hernández	(2) Den. by Manuel Gil de la Guardia (a rec. prisoner)
168	1600	261	91pp	*Puebla* 7 a	Diego Carmona	Rejected for position of Familiar
169	1601	263		1	Diego Hernández Victoria	Letters about his property
170	1601	263	80pp	Manila 1U	Ruipo and his sons (Port.)	(3) Letters from S. O. about them
171	1602	267	3pp	Manila 30	María de Zarate, widow of Diego Hernández Victoria	Letter to S. O. about dec'd's property
172	1603	271	16pp	1	Ruy Diaz Nieto Isabel Rodríguez Violante Rodríguez Sebastian de la Peña Antonio Ruiz Marquez Antonio Méndez Hector de Fonseca Jorge Fernández	(2) Testimony of Duarte (2) Rodríguez concern- (2) ing all the people (2) under this entry (2) (2) (2) (2)
173	1603	271	8pp	6 a	Letter of S. O. that Edict of Faith and Apostolic Brief of Pope Paul be read	
174	1604	273	3pp	16	Antonia Machado, daughter of Dr. Machado and granddaughter of Antonio Machado, rel. est. for being a Jew	Pro., for wearing silk clothes with fringes of gold
175	1604	274	11pp	2	Antonio Fernández (Port.)	(3) Pro., r. *Tlaxcala*
176	1604	274	5pp	11	Francisco Machado, alias Francisco Rodríguez de Molina, grandson of Antonio Machado, rel. est. for being a Jewish dogmatist	Pro., for wearing silk which was prohibited for him
178	1604	274	6pp	12	Alonso Romero del Campo (rec. by Inq. of Cuenca for being a Jew)	Pro. (notary public), for wearing silk clothing, riding a horse, and carrying arms

No.	Year	Vol.	Pages	Document No.	Name of Accused or Document	Charge and Comments
179	1604	274	3pp	18	Rodrigo del Campo (rec. as a Jew, 1603)	Pro., for riding a horse with saddle and bit
180	1605	275	39pp	5 a	Report of the cases disposed of in the *auto de fé*, Mar. 28, 1605 in the Convent of Santo Domingo (Easter Sunday)	
181	1605	276	81pp	14	Ruy Diaz Nieto Hector de Fonseca Isabel Rodríguez Diego Diaz Nieto Antonio Méndez Sebastian de la Peña Antionio Díaz Marquez Sebastián Rodríguez Catalina Rodríguez Constanza Rodríguez (Port.) Violante Rodríguez Ruy Díaz de Lemos Ruy Díaz Nieto (son Marcos) Antonio Rojas Alonso Rojas	Dec. of Manuel Gil de la Guardia and jail warden against all the accused in this entry. *Curious information about Jews*
182	1605	277	14pp	2	Ruy Díaz Manuel Gil Pedro Jorge Rodrigo del Campo Francisco López Enríquez	(2) Denunciation (2) Denunciation (2) Denunciation (2) Denunciation (2) Denunciation
183	1606	277	2pp	6C	Isabel Rodríguez Costanza Rodríguez Justa Méndez Ana Enríquez Tomas Day Antonio López	Den. for not using sambenito Den. for not using sambenito Den. for not using sambenitos Den. for not using sambenitos Den. for not using sambenitos Den. for not using sambenitos
184	1606	277	3pp	7	Sebastian Rodríguez	Pro., Port., for not using sambenitos
185	1606	277	3pp	7A	Costanza Rodríguez	Pro., for not complying with penitence
186	1614	278	pp276-289	*Celaya* 12	Isabel Duarte Leonor Vasquez Ines García Juana Diaz Machorro (Port.) Mencia Meléndez	Test. regarding procesos Test. regarding procesos Test. regarding procesos Test. regarding procesos Test. regarding procesos

No.	Year	Vol.	Pages	Document No.	Name of Accused or Document	Charge and Comments
187	1614	278	pp295-316	*Queré-taro* 14	Pedro Muñoz de la Roja Ana de Silva Maria Vasquez Ana Pérez Francisco Rodríguez Isabel Duarte Francisco Rodríguez	Letter of S. O. in *Querétaro.* Den. for sorcery Sold his soul to the devil
188	1606	279	15pp	9	Sebastian Rodríquez Antonio Méndez Sebastian de la Peña Ruy Diaz Nieto A. Guerrero Marco Antonio Jorge Fernández Antonio López Hector Fonseca Antonio Gómez Duarte Rodríguez Costanza Rodríguez Isabel Rodríguez Clara Enríquez, mother & daughters Ana López Isabel Machado (rec. 1601)	Request to go free in accordance with the grace extended to them by Pope Clement VIII
189	1606	280	Entire Vol.	a̲	This volume contains divers declarations about different matters concerning various individuals. Recourse must be had to volume for further information.	

Tomo 2 (95 pages) covers Volumes 281 to 320 of the Documents.

[Inexplicably it begins with p407 and the original indexer noted that it was badly paginated.]

No.	Year	Vol.	Pages	Document No.	Name of Accused or Document	Charge and Comments
190	1605	281	p585	25	Diego Benitez	Request to open a stall by one rec.
191	1605	281	pp632-635	39	María Rodríguez	(1) Inf. by Franciscan monk
192	1605	281	pp659-662	*Puebla* 47	Manuel López	(4) Testimony
193	1605	281	pp713-714	*Puebla* 61	Gonzalo de Tal (Port.) Alonso González (Port.)	Servants of Alonso de Rivera for practicing certain Jewish acts
194	1608	283	pp87-93	14 a̲	Authority given to Familiar of S. O. in *Guadalajara* to make an investigation of the genealogy of Francisco Rodríguez Carvallo	
195	1608	283	pp266-268	*Zacatecas* 38	Jerónimo Enriquez	(3) Test.
196	1608	283	p297	*Puebla* 49	Heronimo Perez de Salazar	(4) Test.

No.	Year	Vol.	Pages	Document No.	Name of Accused or Document	Charge and Comments
197	1608	283	p352	68 a	D. Frutos Gómez Casillas	Dean of *Chiapas;* letter that he is not "clean"
198	1609	285	pp78-80	*Guatemala* 8	Antonio de Carbajal	For observing Jewish rites
199	1609	285	p164	*Zacatula* 41	Manuel Rodríguez	(3) Den.
200	1609	285	p274	*Chiapas* a 64	Pedro Ortes de Velasco	Father of Dean of Cathedral of *Chiapas,* for impure blood
201	1609	285	p279	67	Antonio Gómez (rec.)	Petition to go to Amozoc to arrange his affairs
202	1610	287	11pp	*Tlaxcala* 6	Gonzálo Pérez Caldero	(2) Pro., r. of *Huejotzingo*
203	1629	289		*Pánuco* 3A	Francisco Rodríguez	(2) He is mentioned in document concerning Edict of Faith in *Pánuco*
204	1620*	289	2pp	*Veracruz* 9P	Rafael Granada Gabriel de Granada	Letter asking for permission to go to Spain and there complete their penitence
205	1611	291	40pp	*Taxco* 5	Juan de Figueroa	(2) Inf. from Comisario of *Taxco*
206	1611	292	p21	6	Luis Pérez Meléndez (an Asturian)	Letter from Comisario of *Michoacán* that he had scolded him
207	1611	292	p215	*Guatemala* 45	An unnamed Portuguese	(1) Inf.
208	1613	293	pp113, 114	Manila 21	Francisco Vaez	Letter from Bishop of Japan announcing arrival of the young man who had been rel. est. by S. O.
209	1614	293	p164	Manila 28	Juan Méndez Esporan and his mother	(Manila). He, at point of death, denounced himself and his mother for practicing Jewish ceremonies
210	1614	293	p165	Manila 29	María Zaldiva	(2) Test.
211	1612	296	4pp	*Cuautla* 11A	Juan Xímon	(3) Palmister and surgeon of Sosa

*An obvious error because all subsequent events were after 1642. Date more likely is c. 1650.

No.	Year	Vol.	Pages	Document No.	Name of Accused or Document	Charge and Comments
212	1613	298	12pp	6	Simón Díaz, son of Manuel Díaz (relaxed), and Isabel Rodríguez (rec.)	For using silks and riding a horse
213	1614	301	3pp	*Jalapa* 10A	Fray Francisco Hurtado	Accused by Comisario of *Jalapa* of being son of relaxed and of apostasy
214	1614	301		*Antequera* 21	Mathías Pérez	(3) Letter from Comisario of *Guadalajara*
215	1614	301	1p	*Tlaxcala* 42A	Jusepe Renaldos	(3) Den. & that he was not baptized
216	1614	301	6pp	*Cuautla* 54	Cristobal Noguera	(3) Testimony
217	1614	302	2pp	*Pachuca* a 8E	Domingo de Figueroa (Port.)	For saying that Moors and Jews did better by confessing only to God
219	1614	302	7pp	*Taxco* 11	Manuel Duarte Ana Roja Tomás Cardoso	Blasphemy. Test. Superstition. Test. (2) Testimony
220	1614	303	p394	67	Gregorio Fajardo	(3) Test.
221	1616	304	p205	*Michoacán* 29	Juan Flores	(4)
222	1615	308	12pp	1	Gonzálo de Molina (grandson of Antonio Machado, relaxed)	Test. Using silk, sword, and riding a horse
223	1615	308	pp322, 333,335	*Querétaro* 35	Francisco Rodríguez	Test. against accused
224	1615	308	pp322-326,330	*Querétaro* 39	María Torres	Test. against accused
225	1615	308	pp334	41	Núñez de Rosa	Test. against accused
226	1615	308	pp562-568	*Guatemala* 96	Juan López Bravo	(4)
227	1615	309	24pp	*Zacatecas* 4	Cristobal de Herrera	(3) Inf. and for teaching the Law of Moses to the Indians
228	1642	311	134pp	2	Da. Isabel Tristán, widow of Luis Fernández Tristán (he was a captain and also her uncle)	(7) b. Seville. Tormented and relaxed (p313). At p325 there is the etymology of Tristán
229	1616	312	p54	11	Manuel Fernández	(3) Inf.
230	1616	312	p190	40	Tinoco (Port.)	Test. that he did not eat pork when he had guests

No.	Year	Vol.	Pages	Document No.	Name of Accused or Document	Charge and Comments
231	1616	313	50pp	5	María de Espinoza, wife Francisco Rodríguez	Letter from Inq. of Llerena with Inf. about María de Espinoza (lived near *Querétaro*)
232	1617	315		5c 5c	Gaspar Rodríguez Anton Pérez	(4) Den., Port. (4) Den., Port.
233	1617	316	pp398-426	*Zacate-cas* 22	Diego López	(4) and irreverence
234	1617	316	pp547-555	*Tepuz-tlán* 37	Alonso Cubas	(4) Test.
235	1618	317	1p	32	Diego Felipe	(4) Test.
236	1618	320	pp419-441	13	Pedro López (Port.)	(3) Pro., criminal

Tomo 3 (95 pages) covering Volumes 321 to 368 inclusive.

No.	Year	Vol.	Pages	Document No.	Name of Accused or Document	Charge and Comments
237	1620	328	p128	*Durango* <u>a</u>	Bartolome del Barco	For having copied witch craft from a book *The Key of Solomon*
238	1620	333	10pp	*Colima* <u>a</u> 40	Simón López de Olivares	Letter from Presiding Justice at *Colima*. Accused called another, "Dog of a Jew"
239	1622	335	1p	41	Francisco Victoria Barahona	Bigamy, and he had been punished in Peru for judaizante
240	1622	335	4pp	*Acapulco* 42	Jorge de Orta	(2) Test.
241	1622	335	1p	86	Draft of a letter denouncing the existence of a synagogue on Santo Domingo Street	
242	1621	337	94pp	*Guatema-la* 7	Manuel Díaz Enríquez (Port.) Pedro Silva Saucedo (Port.)	(2) Pro., criminal
243	1621	339	1p	42	Francisco de Espinoso, son of Simón Rodríguez, a penitent	Den. by Cristobal de Espinosa, for wearing silk
244	1620	341	46pp	7	Draft of a letter from S. O. to the Supreme Council of Inq. in Spain referring to *Jews*, Dutch, and Filipinos	
245	1622	343	26pp	*Xicayau* 19	Cristobal de Alarcon	Inf. he circumcised his son
246	1623	344	350pp	*Nicaragua* 1	Jerónimo Salgado (rel. est. 1626)	(2) Pro., lived in *Granada, Nic.*

No.	Year	Vol.	Pages	Document No.	Name of Accused or Document	Charge and Comments
247	1623	344	50pp	*Guadala-jara* 2	Diego Fuentes, alias Diego Duarte or Juan Flores	(2) Pro.
248	1623	344	49pp	4	Gaspar de Pereira	(2) Pro., b. Bayona
249	1623	345	2pp	*Chiapas* 32	Andres de Acosta, dead	Letter from D. Diego Pinos, Comisario of S. O., declaring Acosta and all his descendants to be Jews
250	1623	345	9pp	*Chiapas* 37	Diego Ome (Port.)	Den. and Inf. because he said he was to be washed (as a Jew) when he died
251	1623	345	60pp		Captain Pedro de Roja, Juana de la Cueva his wife, Alvaro Diez de Lineo, (grandson of Juan García el Conde and María Alonso)	Letter from Inq. Court of Valladolid, Spain, accompanying Inf. and genealogy of those listed in adjoining column. [Note: the original indexer placed the word "judaizantes" at the end of the entry.] Inf. also about the result of the case against Gonzálo Enríquez de Lineo, condemned by his own confession before the Inq. at Llerena
252	1624	347	pp344-497	a	Book of letters to and from Inq. in Mexico to Council of the Grand Inquisitors in Spain from 1571 to 1624 together with its own alphabetical index	
253	1624	348	pp167-549	5	Diego Pérez de Alburquerque (rec. 1630)	(2) Pro. (b. Bordeaux, France)
254	1624	349	pp1-15	*Taxco*	Tómas Fonseca	Accounting & acts about his property
255	1624	349	pp31-193	4	Marcos del Valle, alias Simón López	(2) Criminal cause
256	1623	350	pp28-371	4	Antonio de Medina	(2) Test. & criminal cause
257	1625	353	pp312-320	23	Manuel Xuárez (Port.)	(4) Accused from *Cartagena*
258	1626	354	pp97-101	*Guat.*	Antonio Prieto de Villegas	(1) Test., prisoner in *Cartagena*
259	1626	355	pp225-287	11	Diego Lozada	(2) Inf. Document in bad condition

No.	Year	Vol.	Pages	Document No.	Name of Accused or Document	Charge and Comments
260	1626	356	p34	*Tepeaca*	Francisca Mejía	(3) Test. 2d part
261	1626	356	p77	*Tepeaca*	Isabel de Carrión	(2) 2d part of testimony. Removal of landrecilla
262	1626	356	p155		Diego de León	Test. Being a descendant of Jews, 2d part
263	1626	356	p156	*Zacatecas*	Isabel Rodríguez Castaño	Test. Being a descendant of Jews, 2d part
264	1626	356	p157	*Zacatecas*	Diego Gómez Pereira	Port., for being circumcised
265	1626	356	p175	*Guadalajara* 105	Diego de Lozada	(1) Test., only 2d part
266	1626	356	p260	N. Mex.	Juan Gómez	For words interpreted as those of Jews
267	1627	360	p84		Pedro de Tal	(1) Test.
268	1627	360	p88	Granada	Isabel de Mercado	(3) Test.
269	1627	360	p88	Granada	Felipa de Mercado	(3) Test.
270	1626	360	p88	Granada	Da María de Mercado Da Isabel de Mercado Da Felipa de Mercado	Letter to Granada written by Ruiz de Cordova to his aunts and their replies, said aunts being suspected of being Jews
271	1627	360	pp181-195		Antonio García Cabezuelo	(3) Test.
272	1627	360	p441	*S. Felipe Sinaloa*	Francisco Aliaya Cardona	(1) Test.
273	1627	360	p558	*Campeche*	Rufina González	For removing the landrecilla
274	1627	360	p564	*Puebla*	Juan Jiménez Piquero	(4) Silversmith, Test.
275	1627	360	p564	*Puebla*	Francisco Lucena or Ugena	(1) Test.
276	1627	360	p567	*Guatemala*	Duarte Gómez	(3) Port. - Test.
277	1626	362	p106	*Xalapa*	Luis Alvarez de Acosta (Port.)	(2) Criminal case—Accused from Los Reyes, Peru (see 282)
278	1627	362	pp113-130	*Telita*	Gaspar Díaz (Port.)	(2) Criminal case. - Pro.
279	1628	365	4pp	*Michoacán* 11	Tomás Treviño de Sobremonte	Letter from Fray Alonso Enríquez de Toledo accompanying Test.
280	1628	365	6pp	*Zacatecas* 24	Francisco de Villegas	(4) Pro., and letter of Lic. Diego de Herrera Arteaga, Comisario in *Zacatecas*

No.	Year	Vol.	Pages	Document No.	Name of Accused or Document	Charge and Comments
281	1628	365	6pp	33	Tomás Treviño de Sobremonte	Order of S. O. to Comisario in *Oaxaca* concerning accused's property
282	1630	366	60pp	Lima 4	Antonia de Medina Pedro de Medina Francisco de Acosta Silvao Vergara Luis de Acosta Francisco de Amezquita Jorge Diaz de Montoya	(2) Test. of Francisco (2) de Victoria Barahona, rec. by the (2) hona, rec. by the (2) Inq. at Peru, against (2) all these accused (2) (2) Pro., emanated from Inq. at Goa (written in Portuguese)
283	1629	366	10pp	*Texcuco*	Simón de Paredes (son of Manuel Lucena) Clara Méndez Justa Méndez Pedro Enríquez	(2) Den. and letter from S. O. Comisario in *Texcuco*
284	1629	366	1p	*Huejutla* 35	Francisco Rodríguez	(3) Den.
285	1639-1640	367		4	Alonso López (Port.)	(4) Test.
286	1604	368	p50, 56	S. *Felipe* 9	Pedro de Lima	(3) Test.
287	1604	368	p221	56	Cristobal Miguel	Pro., wearing of silk by rec.
288	1604	368	p227	*Tabasco* 58	Manuel Núñez (Port.)	(2) Test.
289	1604	368	pp299-310	*Aguascalientes* 78	Juan García de Santa Ana, alias Juan García de la Soria	(3) Den.
290	1604	368	p321	a	* *Fulano* Romero (pen.)	For wearing silk and riding horse
291	1604	368	p322		Jorge Vaez de Lemus	(3) Pro.
292	1604	368	p378	93	Alonso de Rojas	Test. for having removed the landrecilla from the leg of the animal
293	1604	368	412	105 a	Antonio López (rec.)	Test. for not having completed his punishment
294	1604	368	p446	112	P. Camargo P. Altamirano	Test., both were sons of Lorenzo Angelo, relapsed, and his wife rec. by Inq. of Llerena

Fulano is not a proper name—it signifies "not known."

No.	Year	Vol.	Pages	Document No.	Name of Accused or Document	Charge and Comments
295	1604	368	pp447-453	113	Antonio Herrera	(2) Imprisoned in *Acapulco* Test.
296	1604	368	pp20-25		Isabel Benitez	Den. for wearing silk, being disqualified

Tomo 4 covers Volumes 369 to 437 inclusive (93 pages).

No.	Year	Vol.	Pages	Document No.	Name of Accused or Document	Charge and Comments
297	1642	369	15pp	16	María de Rivera, widow of Manuel de Granada Margarita de Rivera, sister of María *et al*. (See Pro. of Gabriel de Granada)*	(2) Den. Imprisoned (2) (2) Den. Imprisoned
298	1642	371	20pp	3	Da Blanca Enríquez and her daughters María and Isabel (Belica)	Letters exchanged between the prisoners while in the secret jail of the Inq.
299	1630	372	9pp	3	Baltazar de Ubago	Inf. for saying that the house in Tacubaya of Inquisitor Pedro Bazas was built by the bribes of Jewish Familiars
300	1632	372	35pp	21	Diego Núñez (Port.), brother María de Leon, sister	(2) Case (alias Pacheco) (2) Case
301	1632	372	28pp	26	Amaro Diaz Mataraña	(2) Pro., husband of Margarita Moreyra
302	1631	373	78pp	*Oaxaca* 9	a Alonso Careaje a Gerónimo de Reyna	Pro., for having tried to obstruct the publication of the Edict of Faith. At *pp39* & 62 of Vol. 373, reference is made to the goods of *Tomas Treviño*
303	1631	373		13	Juan González	(8) Den. against him and family
304	1633	373		19	a Pedro Barrientos a Diego Barrientos	Test. for having Jewish ancestors Test. for having Jewish ancestors

PAJHS, No. 7, 1899. The original proceso was owned by Col. David Fergusson, a Scotsman. He took it out of Mexico in 1883 and it was part of twelve boxes of original "Inquisition Documents" destroyed by fire in 1888 (*ibid.*, p. VI).

No.	Year	Vol.	Pages	Document No.	Name of Accused or Document	Charge and Comments
305	1633	373		28	Gaspar Gerónimo	Legal complaint by Francisco Rodríguez and Justa Méndez for calling them "Jew dogs"
306	1632	374	54pp	6	Melchor Xuárez	(1) (2) Pro. and for bigamy
307	1632	375	39 pp	1	Diego López Rivera	(2) Pro. deceased (b. Casteloblanco)
308	1632	375	8pp	3	Melchor Ortega	(2) Pro.
309	1632	376	2pp	2	Francisco Márquez de Leon and his father (not named)	(3) Den. by Da. Catalina Ortiz, wife of accused (Port.)
310	1632	376	7pp	*Comayafua* 6	Pedro Rodríguez Matus	(1) Den. by Precentor of Cathedral
311	1637	376	1p	*Michoacán* 27	Francisco de Fondevilla (Port.)	(4) Letter, accusation from Comisario in *Michoacán*
312	1634	377	12pp	20	Melchor Rodríguez (Port.)	Concealer of Jews (b. *Puebla*)
313	1634	378	341pp	*Pachuca* 1	Antonio Fernández Cardado	(2) Pro., Port.
314	1634	378	174pp	2	Francisco Blandon son of Leonor Núñez, brother-in-law of Tremiño	(2) Relapsed; Contains much Inf. about Jews, especially about Tremiño de Sobremonte
315	1654	379	269pp		Leonor Núñez	(2) 2 Procesos
316	1634	380	239pp	1	Baltazar del Valle Isabel Cardado	(2) (2)
317	1634	381	85pp, also pp450/ 466	5 & 7	Isabel Núñez, wife of Luis Pérez Roldan	(2) see 318
318	1632- 1635	381		5	Violante Méndez Leonor Núñez (b. Madrid) Francisco López Blandon Duarte de León (b. Casteloblanco) Simon Montero Baltazar Diez Isabel López Cardado Antonio Fernández Cardado Marcos del Valle María Gómez (b. Mex. City)	(2) Report (2) Report (2) Report (2) Report (2) Report (2) Report (2) Report (2) Report (2) Report (2) Report

No.	Year	Vol.	Pages	Document No.	Name of Accused or Document	Charge and Comments
					Tomas Tremiño de Sobremonte	(2) Report
					Isabel Núñez	(2) Report
					Ana Gómez	(2) Report
					Ana Gómez Portillo	(2)
					Joseph Baez	(2)
					Manuel Zuárez	(2)
					Ana Fernández	(2)
					Pedro López, a/k/a Simon Fernández	(2)
					Antonio López Blandon	(2)
					María Rodríguez	(2)
					Nicolas de la Raspiera	(2)
					Domingo Hernández	(2)
					Fray Benito Olivares	(2)
					Tomas de Suasnabar y Aguirre	(2)
319	1635	381	10pp	7	Juana Enríquez	(2) Test.
					Simón López	(2) Test.
					Rafael Silva	(2) Test.
					Elena Silva	(2) Test.
					Juana Enríquez	(2) Test.
					Isabel de Silva	(2) Test.
320	1634-1646	381	424pp	9	María Gómez, wife of Tomás Treviño de Sobremonte	(2) Test. 65pp and Pro. criminal 359pp (rec. 1635)
321	1635	382		4	Ana Fernández, dec'd	Test. against her memory and reputation
				a	[Indexer notes that Nos. 5 to 17 are important but reveals no further information.]	
322	1628	383	11pp	18	Gonzálo Barrassa	(2) Pro., Port.
323	1633	385	10pp	Guadalajara 18	a Dr. Gerónimo de Santoyo	Den. by the Dean of Guadalajara because, during a sermon, he preached that in Spain the rich were called Jews
324	1639	386		Sinaloa 2	Gaspar Lorenzo	(1) Letter from P. D. de Guzman, S. J., and Comisario of Sinaloa
325	1639	387	42pp	16	Thomás Núñez (b. Villa de Bayona, Galicia)	(7) Confessed formal doubts of the Catholic Faith and in the mysteries of the Most Holy Altar
326	1639	388	132pp	1	Francisco de Acosta (Port.)	(2) Pro. (all in Portuguese). Had lived in Cartagena
327	1639	388	12pp	Cartagena 7	Alvaro López Mesa	(2) Pro.

No.	Year	Vol.	Pages	Document No.	Name of Accused or Document	Charge and Comments
328	1639	388	27pp	*Zacatecas* 10	Tomás Rodríguez Sobremonte	(1) Den. and papers sent by Comisario of *Zacatecas*
329	1639	388	17pp	*Truxillo*	Antonio de Huerta (Port.) Esteban Adame & Ana de Biedma	(2) Papers of 2 officials in *Truxillo* These 2 were accused of illegal friendship with Huerta, the Jew
330	1640	389	30pp	8	Beatriz Enríquez Leonor Martinez Pedro Tinoco Manuel Acosta (b. Lisbon) Ana Núñez Antonia Núñez Clara Núñez Manuel Méndez de Miranda Francisco Nieto Ramos (b. Casteloblanco; merchant) Juan Duarte Clara Texosa Luis Mezquita Sarmiento, alias Amezquita Sarmiento Juan Martín de la Calle Baltasar Márques Palomo Antonio Fernández Cardado	Test. about the criminals who had gone to Spain. [*Compiler's note:* nothing in the original *Indice* indicated that these "reos" (criminals) were Jews. Later entries verify that.]
331	1640	389	13pp	*Guadiana* 10	Ana Gómez	Report from *Guadiana* and testimony about the recovery of goods confiscated from accused, a rec.
332	1640	389	5pp p522	*Taxco* 12A	Don de Oliver and Antonia de Rivera, his wife	(4) Letter from Comi- (4) sario of *Taxco* with Inf.
333	1641	390	17pp	11	Blanca Méndez Margarita Juana, wife of Simón Baez Manuel Acosta, merchant Gaspar Vaez Juana de León Diego Corre Miguel Núñez Andres Almeyda	Test. of Gaspar de Robles
334	1641	390	11pp	Lima 18	Diego Calvo (Port.)	(7) Pro.
335	1641	391	111pp	1	Francisco Home, alias Vicente Henriquez	(2) C. C. Married his niece, María Henriquez, was

No.	Year	Vol.	Pages	Document No.	Name of Accused or Document	Charge and Comments
					Beatriz Hernández, his mother Justa Henriquez, his aunt Beatriz Rodríguez, his aunt Justa Montes, his aunt Francisca Núñez, his aunt Gaspar Méndez Piñeiro, his brother (b. San Vicente Davera) Henrique de Miranda, his brother Pedro López, his brother Gaspar de Robles, his nephew Francisco Núñez, his nephew Juan de Roxas, his nephew Domingo Rodríguez Isabel Núñez Francisco Nieto (married Clara Fernández in Seville, & Leonor Núñez in Mex. City)	denounced by his nephew, & under torment admitted that he & others under his name in adjoining column were Jews. He was crippled as a result of the torture and died in jail.
336	1647	391	8pp	2	Thomas del Rincón Francisco de Peñalosa Betanzos Lic. Pedro Núñez de Luna	(2) Inf. from *Temascaltepec;* Rincón is the Vicar, & de Luna the Curator, accused by things they said
337	1642	391		10	Beatriz Méndez Guimor Núñez Ana Rodríguez Gonzalo Vaez María Henriquez Catalina Rivera Maldonado Francisco Oporto Francisco López de Altavista Isabel Enríquez María Enriquez Luis de Mena Antonio Rodríguez Núñez Guimor Rodríguez Isabel Rodriguez Clara Henriquez P. López Home Diego Vaez Francisca López de Fonseca	Test. against the people all now dead. (In the list, referring to Vol., are the places where they died.) [*Compiler's note:* the date 1642 is in error since many were in the *autos* from 1646 to 1649]

No.	Year	Vol.	Pages	Document No.	Name of Accused or Document	Charge and Comments
					Gaspar Méndez (r. *Guadalajara*) Esperanza Rodríguez Beatriz Fernández Antonio de Granada Fernándo Vaez Tórres Rafael Gómez (Texoso; b. Valencia; bachelor; broker) Blanca Méndez, alias Blanca de Rivera (b. Seville; rec. 1646) Clara Núñez Diego López Blanca de Gama Andres de Almeida Domingo López Beatriz López Diego López	
338	1642	392	35pp	3	Jorge Jacinto Bazán (b. Malaga) & Blanca Suarez, his wife	Inventory & sequestra- tion of property
					Diego Rodríguez Arias	Who lived in their house
					Jorge Xacinto (Note Jorge Jacinto Bazan)	Auction of his clothing
					Diego Rodríguez Arias	Auction of his clothing
339	1642	392	44pp	5	Gaspar Suárez Rafaela Enriquez	Inventory & sequestra- tion of their property
340	1642	392	2pp	6	Juana Duarte de Espinoza	Note or account payable of Gregorio de Saldaña for 14 pesos
341	1642	392	10pp	7	Juan Duarte Thomas Núñez de Peralta	Order of arrest and ac- tions for sequestra- tion of their property
342	1643	392	19pp	12	Jorge Jacinto, merchant Blanca Xuárez, daughter of Gaspar Xuárez	Acts to recapture the slaves of the ac- cused from Diego de Mendoza
343	1644	392	16pp	13	A proceeding by the Officials of the Royal Treasury against Jorge Jacinto for 10 pesos for 4 gallons of wine of Simón Vaez and another for 1 peso 216 reales	
344	1644	392	2pp	16	A proceeding similar to 343 to recover 36 pesos from Jorge Jacinto for the property of Juan Méndez	
345	1644	392	17pp	17	Juan Rodríguez Xuárez	Demand for 35 pesos for rent

No.	Year	Vol.	Pages	Document No.	Name of Accused or Document	Charge and Comments
346	1645	392	6pp	22	Royal Treasury suit against Juan Duarte for 18 pesos 6 tomines (reals) which belonged to Thomas Treviño	
347	1642	393	461pp	1 & 2	Da. Beatriz Enríquez, wife of Thomas Nuñez de Peralta, (b. New *Veracruz*)	Test. & Pro. in 2 parts
348	1642	393	84pp	3	Juan Duarte Isabel de la Huerta, daughter of Juan Méndez and Juan Méndez, himself María Arias, mother of Leonor de Rojas Nuño de Pereyra (Port.) Enrique Fernández Diego Díaz Clara Antunez, daughter of Isabel Duarte Manuel Antunez, son of Isabel Duarte Clara Texosso (r. *Veracruz*) Isabel Texosso Duarte Rodríguez Diego Méndez de Silva Gaspar Alfaro María de Rivera	(2) Test. of Da. Isabel de Silva
349	1642	393	22pp	4	Isabel de Rivera	(2) Test. of Miguel de Almonacir
350	1642	393	28pp	5	Manuel de Segovia D. Guillen Lombardo de Guzman	(2) Test. of Isabel de Silva
351	1642	393	71pp	6	Justa Méndez	Test. of Blanca de Rivera
352	1642	393	17pp	7	Da. Ana de Campos Sebastian Vaez Acevedo	Test. of Isabel de Silva
353	1642	393	12pp	9	Da. Isabel de Espinosa	(2) Test. of Blanca de Rivera
354	1642	393	6pp	10	Leonor Vaez María Arias Francisco López, bachelor	Test. of Gaspar de Vaez. Bad—destroyed by dampness
355	1642 1656	394	126pp 160pp	1	Diego Díaz	(2) Pro. (2) 1st in 1642 and 2d in 1656
356	1642	394	190pp	2	Margarita de Rivera	(2) Pro., 1st part
357	1642	394	121pp	3	Violante Suárez	(2) Pro. and C. C.
358	1642	395	25pp	1	Pedro Mercado	(2) Pro., b. Madrid, heretical

No.	Year	Vol.	Pages	Document No.	Name of Accused or Document	Charge and Comments
359	1642	395	132pp	2	Agustín de Roxas, dec'd, husband of Leonor de Rojas or Leonor Vaez	(2) Pro., and C. C. Hung himself in jail. (Rel. est. with his bones 1649)
360	1642 1668	395	198pp 81pp	3 & 4	Melchor Rodríquez López	(2) Merchant, b. Villa de Cobillán. Pro. and C. C.
361	1642	395	265pp	5	Thomas Núñez de Peralta (also conspirator of Don Guillermo Lampart)	(7) At p245, he asked to be permitted to go to hospital because he was sick and his cell flooded
362	1642	396	254pp	1	Isabel de Rivera	(2) Pro. For whipping a statue of Christ
363	1642	396	229pp	2	Bachiller Pedro Tinoco	(2) Doctor
364	1642	396	62pp	3	Francisco de la Cruz, slave of Simón Vaez of Seville; Antonia de la Cruz, Negress (slave of Thomas Núñez de Peralta) & Isabel, Negress (b. in America, slave of Simón Vaez)	[Note: The Indexer wrote a lengthy entry which indicates that the slaves were carrying communications within the secret cells of the Inq., and there is a list of the prisoners who "squealed"]
365	1642	396	39pp	4	Da. Blanca, Da. María, Da. Isabel, Da. Clara, Da. Catalina, Da. Isabel de Rivera, mother and daughters	[These prisoners were also exchanging communications and their messages were intercepted.] In jail for heretical Jewish practices.
366	1642	396	15pp	5	Pedro López Home	(7) Died in *Guadalajara*
367	1642	397	258pp	2	Da. Micaela Enríquez, wife of Sebastian Cardoso. (b. Seville)	(2) Testimony of 75 Jews
368	1642	397	212pp	3	Luis de Olivares Ricio (Port.). Acquitted and exonerated.	(2) His son, Capt. Luis Olivares, came to his defense and completely proved that his father was neither Port. nor Jew and that some Jews had denounced the accused for revenge
369	1642	398	295pp	1	Simón Vaez de Sevilla	(7) b. Santiago, Castille; educated in Casteloblanco

No.	Year	Vol.	Pages	Document No.	Name of Accused or Document	Charge and Comments
370	1642	398	22pp	2	Manuel Coronel, fugitive	(2) Pro., heretical, b. Villa de Camina, Port.
371	1642	398	28pp	3	Felipe López de Nóroña	(2) Husband of Clara de Rivera, Pro.
372	1642	398	24pp	4	Enrique de Miranda, brother of Violante Enrique, alias Francisco Home	(1) Pro., Port.
373	1642	399	168pp	1	Leonor de Rojas, alias Vaez, wife of Augustin de Roxas	(7) Pro. Tormented and then confessed
374	1642	399	92pp	Puebla a 2	Sebastian Domingo, alias Munguía, Negro slave of Luis de Mesquita (Port.), a foreman or overseer)	While working in secret cells of Inq. he carried messages to various people. (Luis was b. in Segovia)
375	1642	399	10pp	3	Blanca Enríquez, mother of witness against her	(2) Test. of Juana Enríquez daughter of accused
376	1642	399	23pp	4	Isabel de Rivera	(2) Test. of Fernando de la Fuente
377	1642	399	30pp	5	Isabel de Rivera, daughter of witness	(2) Test. of Blanca de Rivera, mother of accused
378	1642	399	23pp	7	Isabel de Rivera daughter of witness	(2) Test. of Blanca de Rivera, mother of accused
379	1642	399	4pp	9	Manuel de Mella	(2) Test. of Catalina de Rivera
380	1642	399	23pp	10	Juan de Rojas (b. Sebillan, Port.)	(2) Pro., husband of Francisca Núñez
381	1642	399	12pp	11	Da. Catalina Enríquez	Test. of Blanca de Rivera
382	1646	399	21pp	12	Hernándo Rodríguez Jerónimo Fernandez Correa Francisco López Correa Ros. Fernández Correa Thomas Méndez Antonio González Xamayca Gaspar Andrés Manuel Méndez Alberto Duarte Correa Diego Méndez Marino Manuel de Barrios	Report on pending cases in S. O. and their interrelationships and events since 1642

No.	Year	Vol.	Pages	Document No.	Name of Accused or Document	Charge and Comments
					Juan Rodríguez Xuárez Gerónimo Moreno Luis de Olivera Juan Cardoso, alias Gabriel Peregrino	
383	1642	399	2pp	13	Capitan Luis Fernández Tristán	(2) Pro., Port., died at sea
384	1642	399	20pp	16	Gabriel Rodríguez, son of Antonio Rodríguez Arias	(2) Pro., died *Veracruz*. rel. est. 1649
385	1642	400	455pp	1	Da. Juana Enríquez de Silva, wife of Simón Vaez de Sevilla	(7) 2d part of pro. She testified against 114 Jews. She was tortured and confessed on the 2d turn of the wheel. She was regarded as a perfect and saintly Jewess. She fasted, prayed and bathed for all the holidays and gave charity to all who fasted
386	1642	400	392pp	2	Juan Pecheco de León, alias Salomón Machorro	(2) Pro., b. Antequera, Spain; r. *Querétaro*; tortured, confessed
387	1642	401	135pp	1	Isabel Núñez, wife of Duarte de León	(7) Pro. and dragging a statue of Christ
388	1642	401	60pp	2	<u>a</u> File with statement of jail guards about exchange of messages by prisoners	
389	1644-1645	401	60pp	3	Thomás Treviño de Sobremonte Francisco López Blandon Luis Pérez Roldán	Conversations between the prisoners which were heard by Gaspar Alfaro and his cellmate Luis Perez de Vargas
390	1642	401	39pp	4	Miguel de Almonacer Juan Ramos Blanca Méndez María de Rivera Isabel de Rivera & her daughters Luis Núñez Pérez Hernándo de la Fuente Gaspar de Alfaro Diego de Almonacir	Conversations or communications among the jail cells of the imprisoned
391	1642	401	21pp	5	Manuel López Núñez	(2) Pro., b. Seville, merchant

No.	Year	Vol.	Pages	Document No.	Name of Accused or Document	Charge and Comments
392	1642	401	333pp	7	Da. Isabel Tinoco, wife of Manuel Acosta (son of Antonio Acosta & Juana López)	(2) Pro., b. *Zacatecas*
393	1642	402	473pp	1	Da. Raphaela Enríquez (Port.) wife of Gaspar Suárez (Port.)	(7) Pro. 187 Jewish witness testified in this trial
394	1642	402		2	Rafael de Granada, a student of rhetoric (b. *Mexico;* see Riva Palacio Index)	(7) Pro. 15 years of age *Curious information*
395	1642	403	174pp	1	Pedro de Espinosa, husband of Da. Isabel Enríquez de Silva	Pro. For practicing Judaism
396	1642	403	97pp	2	Manuel de Mella, husband of Violante Suárez; merchant	(2) Pro., b. Huelva, Andalucía; r. *Guadalajara*
397	1642	403	272pp	3	Da. María de Rivera, wife of Manuel de Granada and mother of Rafael de Granada	(2) Pro. A 2d offender. Died in prison. Autopsy made. (See Rafael Granada)
398	1642	404	236pp	1	Isabel Espinosa, aunt of witness Simón Fernández Clara de Rivera Isabel de Rivera Miguel Tinoco, her son María Rivera Bartolomé Gómez Enríquez Family Blanca Enríquez (b. Lisbon; r. *Veracruz*) Manuel de Granada (a/k/a Granado; b. Seville; merchant) Simón López Nuño Suárez Francisco López the Flat-nosed (b. Casteloblanco; r. *Zacatecas*) Enrique Fernández Clara Enríquez Simona de Silva Miguel Núñez Huerta María de León Diego Méndez de Silva Manuel Luis de Mezquita, merchant; son of López de Amezquita & Isabel Gómez of Mex. City	Test. of Catalina Enríquez de Silva

No.	Year	Vol.	Pages	Document No.	Name of Accused or Document	Charge and Comments
					Catalina Maldonado	
					Jerónimo Núñez Roxas, bachelor (b. de la Guarda, Port.)	
					Clara de Espinosa	
					Gonzálo López de Aguardia	
					Isabel de Rivera	
399	1642	404	87pp	2	Luis de Olivares	Test. of Clara de Texoso
					María de Rivera	
					Isabel Texoso	
					Catalina Tinoco	
					Violante Rodríguez (b. Lisbon; r. *Veracruz*)	
					Juan Olivares	
					Gabriel Gómez	
					Pedro Gómez Texoso	
					Miguel Núñez	
					Ana de Rivera	
					Duarte Rodríguez	
					Jerónimo Fernández Correa (b. *Veracruz*; r. *Campeche*)	
					Blanca Enríquez (rel. est. with her bones, 1649)	
					Rafael de Granada	
					Fernándo Rodríguez	
400	1642	404	83pp	3	Da. Blanca Enríquez	Test. of Da. Isabel de Silva
					Francisco López, the Flat-Nosed (merchant)	
					Manuel de Granada (died Philippine Islands)	
					Simón Hernán de Torres	
					Isabel Espinosa	
					Leonor Vaez	
					Violante Rodríguez (sister of Luis Fernández Tristan, relajado)	
					Simon Díaz	
401	1642	404	80pp	4	María de Rivera, daughter of witness— beating a statute of Christ	Test. of Blanca Rivera
					Simón Montero (b. Casteloblanco, Port.; merchant)	
					Leonor Núñez	
					Diego Antunez (Port.; merchant; husband of Isabel Duarte)	
					Nuño Suárez	
					Diego de Campo	

No.	Year	Vol.	Pages	Document No.	Name of Accused or Accused	Charge and Comments
					Miguel Núñez Huerta	
					Diego López de Granada	
					Isabel Rodríguez	
					Ana Gómez	
					Francisco Jorge	
					Juan Campos	
					Francisco Botello	
402	1642	404	106pp	5	Miguel Núñez Huerta Antonio Juárez Gaspar Rodríguez Alfaro María Rodríguez Manuel Carrasco (sugar refiner in Valley of Amilpas) Felipe López Gaspar de Robles Diego Méndez de Silva Thome Gómez (b. Casteloblanco; son of Manuel Rodríguez & Catalina Gómez) Enriquez Hernández Isabel de Rivera María de Rivera Isabel de Huerta, alias the Rose Jorge de Montoya (G.O., b. Casteloblanco; M., b. Holland)	Test. of Clara de Rivera
403	1642	404	10pp	6	María de Rivera	Test. of Antonio López de Orduña
404	1642	405	156pp	1	Francisca Núñez, mother of Juan Roxas Alvaro Núñez de Segovia, husband of Cridonia de Campos Manuel Díaz Rojas Simón López de Guardia Manuel Alvarez de Arellano Blanca Enríquez Catalina de Rivera (b. Seville; wife of Diego Correa de Silva) Clara de Rivera Catalina Enríquez	Test. of Da. Margarita Rivera
405	1642	405	76pp	2	Gaspar Núñez Rafael de Granada Gómez de Silva Gaspar Juárez (rec. 1649)	Test. of Gaspar Vaez of Seville

No.	Year	Vol.	Pages	Document No.	Name of Accused or Document	Charge and Comments
					Isabel de Rivera Gabriel de Granada Simon Fernández (b. Gobea, Port.; merchant in *Guadalajara*) Micaela Enríquez Clara de Rivera Manuel de Acosta (rec. 1648) Simon de Espinosa	
406	1642	405	71pp	3	Manuel Núñez de Huerta Gómez de Silva Diego Juárez de Figueroa (refused to eat nonkosher meal in jail) Clara de Rivera Manuel de Mella	Test. of Da. Isabel de Silva
407	1642	405	p306 et seq.	4	Da. Beatriz Texosa, sister of witness Pedro López Tristán Rafael Gómez Texoso (dec'd; rel. est. 1649) Rafael Enríquez Tomás Méndez	Test. of Da. Clara Texoso
408	1642	405	p393	6	Blanca Enríquez, mother of witness	Test. of Da. Elena Tinoco de Enríquez
409	1642	405	p356 et seq.	6a	María de Rivera Pedro Suárez de Figeroa Beatriz Rodríguez Isabel de Espinoza Clara de Silva (b. Seville; died Mex.) Manuel de Granada (rel. est. 1649) Violante Suárez	Test. of Manuel Mella
410	1642	405	p409 et seq.	7	Martín Manuel Coronel (rel. est. 1649)	Test. of Da. Catalina Tinoco Enríquez
					J. de Montoya Diego Tinoco Leonor Vaez	Test. of Da. Catalina Enríquez de Silva
					Gabriel de Granada Clara de Silva	Test. of Manuel Tinoco Test. of Isabel Tinoco
411	1642	405	p422 et seq.	8	Felipe de Burgos	Test. of Da. Beatriz de Enríquez
					Felipe Burgos Antonio Burgos Francisco Méndez	Test. of Da. Rafaela Enríquez

No.	Year	Vol.	Pages	Document No.	Name of Accused or Document	Charge and Comments
					Felipe de Burgos	Test. of López de
					Antonio de Burgos	Fonseca
					Blanca de Rivera	Test. of Beatriz
					Margarita de Rivera	Enríquez
					Blanca Enríquez, daughter of Blanca Enríquez and Fernándo Rios	
					María de Rivera	
412	1642	405	p450	9	Gonzálo Díaz, brother of witness (b. Casteloblanco)	Test. of Baltazar Díaz
			p454		Antonio Rodríguez Arias	
			p458		Clara de Rivera	
			p460		Leonor de Silva	
			p462		María Rivera	
			p464		Margarita de Rivera	
			p466		Blanca de Rivera	
			p469		Blanca Enríquez	
			p472		Francisco Home	Test. of Da. Blanca de
			p475		Juana Rodríguez	Rivera
			p478		Ana Enríquez	
			p485		Manuel López Núñez, brother of Isabel Tristan (rel. est. 1649)	
			p488		Isabel de Campos	
			p492		Alvaro Núñez	
			p496		Tomé Gómez (married Catalina Samaniego; r. *Aguacatlán*)	
			p498		Enrique Fernández	
			p501		Gaspar de Robles	
			p505		Gómez de Silva	
			p509		Esperanza Jerónima (a/k/a Jerónimo Esperanza & Esperanza Jerónima de Silva)	
			p513		Blas de la Peña	
			p516		Francisco López Enríquez (b. Seville)	
			p519		Luis López de Huerta	
			p522		Manuel de Granada	
			p527		Manuel de Mella	
			p531		Juan de Rojas (died prior to being rel. est. 1649)	
			p534		Blanca Enríquez	
			p545		Francisca Núñez (wife of Juan de Rojas, above)	
			p549		Ana Rodríguez	
			p552		Micaela Enríquez	
			p559		Leonor Baez	
			p562		Blanca Rodríguez	
			p565		Inez López	

No.	Year	Vol.	Pages	Document No.	Name of Accused or Document	Charge and Comments
			p569		Tomás de Tremiño	
			p577		Manuel Carrasco	
			p580		Manuel Núñez or Manuel Rodríguez	
			p587		Francisco López, el Chato (rec. 1648) Catalina Enríquez	
			p590		Sebastián Romas, husband of Esperanza Jerónima	
413	1642	405	p592	10	22 pages—No names in Original Index	Test. of Margarita de Rivera
414	1642	406	70pp	1	Texoso (family)	Test. of Isabel Tinoco
			p3		Diego Tinoco	
			p5		Elena de Silva	
			p7		María de Rivera	
			p12		Margarita de Rivera	
			p16		Isabel de Rivera	
			p20		Blanca Méndez	
			p23		Micaela Enríquez	
			p25		Catalina Enríquez	
			p28		Simon de Espinoza	
			p30		Blanca Enríquez	
			p37		Blanca Suárez	
			p40		Da. Jerónima (b. Seville; *dogmatista;* rel. est. 1649)	
			p42		Antonio Tinoco (b. Mex. City; son of Diego Tinoco and Catalina Enríquez	
			p44		Nuño de Silva (b. Mex. City; rec. 1647)	
			p46		Isabel de Espinoza	
			p49		Diego Méndez	
			p51		Isabel de Granada	
			p53		Pedro Fernández de Castro	
			p56		Juan Méndez	
			p60		Isabel Méndez	
			p65		Antonio Rodríguez Arias (b. Seville; broker, later merchant)	
415	1642	406	p71 et seq.		(72 pages of testi- mony without names appearing in Index)	Test. of Blanca de Rivera
			p143		Nuño de Silva	
			p152		Catalina de Silva	
			p286- 353		Isabel de Rivera Margarita de Rivera	
			p354		Isabel de Silva	
			p417		Luis Núñez Pérez	
			p423		Blanca de Rivera	
			p501		Clara de Rivera	

No.	Year	Vol.	Pages	Document No.	Name of Accused or Document	Charge and Comments
			p537		Isabel de Rivera	
			p563		Manuel Carrasco (son of Francisco Rios Carrasco and Felipa López, dec'd)	
			p574		Isabel de Silva	
			p583		Isabel Antunez	
			p586		Manuel Rodríguez Núñez and against other Jews	
			p380		Luis Cañizo Pérez	
416	1642	407	87pp	1	Manuel Carrasco	(7) Pro., b. Villafort, Port.
417	1642	407	pp213-234	3	Papers of S. O. which show that María de la Paz, widow of Francisco de Herrera Campos, brother of Agustín Herrera Campos, was the executor for Francisco Ruiz Marañon, Constable of the secret Jails	
418	1642	407	p235	4	Manuel Ramirez de Portilla	(2) Pro.
419	1642	407	p259	5	Gaspar Vaez & other people	Test. of Catalina de Rivera
420	1642	407	p384	7	Francisco de Campos (b. Seville)	(2) C. C.—*Campeche*
421	1640	407	p392	8	Esperanza Rodríguez, mulato	(2) A recluse in secret jail
422	1642	407	p427	10	Guiomar Enríquez	(2) Pro.
423	1642	407	p438	12	<u>a</u> Letter written by S. O. to Council in Spain relative to the Port.	
424	1642	407	p471	16	Acts resulting from the denunciation by Antonio Tejera de Morais, Port., bookbinder, by reason of a manuscript in a notebook which was delivered for binding entitled "Virtues of Moses"	
425	1643	408	388pp	1	Margarita de Rivera	(2) Pro., 2d part
426	1642	408	70pp	2	Esperanza Rodríguez, mulato (64 years old; daughter of Negro from Guinea & Francisco Rodríguez)	(2) Pro., b. Seville, widow of the German, Juan Bautista del Bosque (sculptor & worker in wood)
427	1642	408	96pp	3	Da. Clara Enríquez or Clara Duarte, Clara Antunez, 15 yrs.	(7) Pro., (note "Moisen"), b. & r. in *Mexico* (Medina says 19 years)
428	1642	408	61pp	4	Nuño de Silva Suárez de Figueroa, son of Diego Suárez de Figueroa (relates mourning practices)	(7) Pro., b. and r. in *Patzcuaro*

No.	Year	Vol.	Pages	Document No.	Name of Accused or Document	Charge and Comments
429	1642	409	212pp	1	Mathías Rodríguez de Olivera (Port.)	(7) Pro., tortured; b. Laenz
430	1642	409	198pp	2	Antonio Caravallo, husband of Da. Isabel de Silva	(2) Pro., tortured
431	1642	409	68pp	3	Diego Méndez de Silva (b. Albur-querque, Port.)	(7) Pro., Confessed un-der torture residing in Mexico
432	1642	409	117pp	4	Pedro Fernández de Castro, alias Juan Fernández de Castro (rec. Jan. 23, 1647)	(7) Pro., lived near the mines of *Chichicapa* (b. Valladolid, Spain)
433	1642	410	267pp	1	Ana Suárez, wife of Francisco López de Fonseca	(2) Pro.
434	1642	410	234pp	2	Francisco Méndez or Francisco López de Fonseca, husband of Ana Xuárez; son of Manuel Gómez Al-varez, burned at stake in Coimbra for Jewish practices	(2) Pro., b. Botán, Port.; r. in *Veracruz*, tor-mented, confessed. Died aboard ship for Spain
435	1642	410	10pp	3	Juan de Torres de Rivera (b. Lisbon)	(2) Pro., traffiker in slaves, drowned him-self in the Philippines, Isle of Boronga
436	1642	410	pp515-536	4	Diego Tinoco, hus-band of Catalina Enríquez	(2) Pro., b. Seville
437	1642	410	p537	5	Gaspar Méndez (dec'd), brother of Vincente Enrique, alias Francisco Home	(2) Pro., b. San Vicente Davera, Port. (rel. est. 1649)
438	1642	411	317pp	1	Gaspar Vaez, son of Simón Vaez of Seville & Da. Juana Enríquez	(7) Pro., b. in *Mexico*, 18 years of age
439	1656	412	415pp	1	Francisco Botello (b. Villa de Priego)	(7) Expenses in Jail (pp199-202) (p203 et seq.) is 2d Pro. He had been relaxed in 1650. Tortured
440	1642	412	pp416	2	Luis Núñez Pérez	(7) A case; attention is called to agreement between Holland & Portugal at p468
441	1642	412	pp553-590	3	Alvaro de Acuña	Test. of Da. Margarita de Rivera

No.	Year	Vol.	Pages	Document No.	Name of Accused or Document	Charge and Comments
441A	1642	413	21pp	19	Test. of Sebastian Cardoso and of Clara de Rivera	
441B	1642	413	p507	19	Francisco Frayle Melchor Rodríguez Luis de la Mezquita Jorge Fernández Diego Fernández	(2) Test. of Nuño de Figueroa, alias Nuño Pereyra (b. Lisbon; merchant in *Guadalajara;* son of Antonio Jabeira & Isabel de Figueroa)
441C	1642	413	279pp		Diego Núñez, merchant *(Querétaro)*	(2) Test. against accused
441D	1642	413	p529	22	Command to imprison Miguel Fernández de Fonseca	
442	1642	413	p587	32	Letter of Fray Fernándo de Alaren relative to places where he had goods of some Portuguese Jews, *Fresnillo*	
443	1642	413	pp3,4		Gaspar Núñez	(2) Test. against accused
444	1642	413	pp5-50		a Declarations of Miguel Almonacir, Notary of Secrets, about the breaking of the secrets of the jail	
445	1642	413	pp51-53 pp95-96 pp131-135 pp196-201 pp271-276 pp286-293		Antonio Vaez Castelo Blanco	(2) Test.
446	1642	413	pp54-60		Rafaela Enríquez	(2) Test.
447	1642	413	pp61-63, 128-130 161-163		Antonio Rodríguez Arias, husband of Blanco Enríquez	(2) Test.
448	1642	413	pp64,65		María Rodríguez del Bosque	(2) Test.
449	1642	413	pp66-73, 298-303		Catalina Enríquez	(2) Test.
450	1645	413	pp74-81		Fernándo Rodríguez (Port.)	(2) Test. (b. Albeiro; dealer in Negro slaves)
451	1642	413	pp82-85		Blas López	(2) Test.
452	1642	413	pp86-88		Gabriel de Granada	(2) Test.
453	1642	413	pp89-91 pp153,154		Rafael de Granada María de Rivera	(2) Test.
454	1642	413	pp92-95		Gaspar de Robledo	(2) Test.
455	1642	413	pp97-100, 165,166		Simón Díaz de Espinoza	(2) Test.
456	1642	413	pp101-104		Francisco Díaz López, el Chato	(2) Test.

No.	Year	Vol.	Pages	Document No.	Name of Accused or Document	Charge and Comments
457	1642	413	pp105-111		Elena López	(2) Test. (Estramadura)
458	1642	413	pp205-258		Catalina de Rivera	(2) Test.
459	1642	413	pp114-115, 250-258		Simón Fernández	(2) Test., son of Diego Antunez de Torres & Isabel Núñez
460	1642	413	pp116-119		Nuño Súarez de Figueroa	(2) Test.
461	1642	413	pp124-127		Blanca Enríquez	(2) Test.
462	1642	413	pp136-140		Gonzálo Flores	(2) Test.
463	1642	413	pp141-147		Manuel Mella	(2) Test.
464	1642	413	pp148-150		Micaela Enríquez	(2) Test.
465	1642	413	pp151-152		Diego Díaz, husband of Ana Gómez	(2) Test. (burned alive 1659)
466	1642	413	pp155,156		Manuel Carrasco	(2) Test.
467	1642	413	pp157,158		Luis de Burgos	(2) Test.
468	1642	413	pp159,160		Francisco Medina	(2) Test.
469	1642	413	pp163,164		Manuel Díaz (b. Rodrigo, Castile), single, peddler	(2) Test., son of Enrique Rodríguez & Felipa Marqueda
470	1642	413	pp167,168, 175-177, 258		Blanca Enríquez	(2) Test.
471	1642	413	pp169,170		Francisco Méndez	(2) Test.
472	1642	413	pp171-174		Diego Antunez	(2) Test. (rel. est. 1649)
473	1642	413	pp178-183		Beatriz López	(2) Test.
474	1642	413	pp184-187, 239-246		Antonio Carvallo	(2) Test.
475	1642	413	pp187,188		Blanca Xuárez	(2) Test.
476	1642	413	pp189-191, 217-219, 265-271		Blanca de Rivera	(2) Test.
477	1642	413	pp169,170		Francisco Méndez	(Repeated in index)
478-481 are a repetition of 472 to 474 inclusive						
482	1642	413			Clara de Rivera	(2) Test. (same pages as 476)
483	1642	413	pp192-195		Gaspar de Alfar	(2) Test.
484	1642	413	pp202-206		Clara Antúnez	(2) Test. (rec. 1646)
485	1642	413	pp206-208		Gaspar Núñez Media	(2) Test., b. Cartajena
486	1642	413	pp209-216, 294-297		Catalina Maldonado	(2) Test.
487	1642	413	pp220-234, 259-264		Isabel Rivera	(2) Test.

No.	Year	Vol.	Pages	Document No.	Name of Accused or Document	Charge and Comments
488	1642	413	pp235-238		Manuel Núñez Carballo	(2) Test.
489	1642	413	pp247-249		Clara Duarte	(2) Test.
490	1642	413	pp277-279		Agustín Rojas	(2) Test.
491	1642	414	p3	1	Clara de Rivera	Test. of Luis Núñez
			p14		María de Rivera	Pérez
			p26		Diego Correa	
			p32		Simón Espinoza	
			p41		Simón de Fonseca	
			p47		Manuel Núñez	
			p53		Antonio Díaz	
			p62		Barbara Tenorio	
			p68		Diego Méndez Silva	
			p71		Juan de Silva	
			p73		Guillermo Correa	
			p80		Gaspar Rodríguez	
			p82		Luis Correa	
			p91		Clara Texoso (rec. 1646)	
			p94		Andres Almeyda	
			p97		Manuel Pérez Carello	
			p102		Catalina	
			pp103,131		Antonio Méndez Chillón (b. Lisbon; son of Francisco Méndez & Beatriz López)	
			p106		Isabel de Huerta	
			p110		Anna Correa	
			p116		Antonio Báez Castillo Blanco	
			p119		Simón de España	
			p122		Manuel de Acosta	
			p125		Luis de Mesquita	
			p128		Maria del Bosque (b. *Guadalajara*; daughter of Esperanza Rodríguez; confessed 1646)	
			p135		Rafael de Granada	
			p141		Gabriel de Granada	
			p144		Jerónimo Correa	
			p138		Manuel de Granada	
492	1642	414	p148	2	Blanca Enríquez	Test. of Manuel Rodrí-
			p150		Nuño Pardo	guez Núñez
			p153		Beatriz Núñez	
			p158		Antonio Vaez Castelo Blanco	
			p160		Blanca Rodríguez	
			p164		Luis Pérez Roldan	
			p167		Diego López Lucena	
			p169		Diego Rodríguez Arias	
			p172		Ana Gómez	
			p177		Isabel Núñez	

No.	Year	Vol.	Pages	Document No.	Name of Accused or Document	Charge and Comments
			p182		Duarte de Torres (b. Casteloblanco; merchant; rec. 1647)	
			p185		Simón Rodríguez	
			p187		Antonio Suárez	
			p189		Manuel Rodríguez Horta	
			p191		Manuel Rodríguez Carballo	
			p195		Francisco Nieto (rec. 1649 with sambenito & loss of property)	
			p197		Pedro de Guevara	
			p202		Luis de la Mezquita	
			p204		Diego Méndez de Silva	
			p206		Manuel Díaz Cantillana	
			p210		Gaspar de Fonseca, alias Méndez (b. Lisbon; r. *Autla;* rel. est. 1649)	
			p213		Francisco Rodríguez Castillo Blanco	
			p219		López Simon	
			p221		Manuel Carrasco	
493	1642	414	p223	3	Francisco López Enríquez	Test. of Da. Rafaela Enríquez
			p227		Simón Fernández	
			p229		Elena Silva	
			p231		D. Suárez de Figueroa	
			p232		Isabel Enríquez, alias Isabel de la Huerta	
			p235		Antonio Tinoco (rel. est. 1649)	
			p237		Manuel Granada	
			p241		Diego Núñez (dec'd; rel. est. with his bones 1649)	
			p243		Clara de Silva, daughter of Blanca Enríquez	
			p245		Clara Enríquez	
			p247		Catalina Enríquez	
			p252		Blanca Suárez	
			p254		Violante Suárez	
			p256		Francisco Núñez	
			p260		Micaela Enríquez	
			p266		Nuño de Silva	
			p271		Miguel Núñez	
			p273		Juan Méndez	
			p275		Isabel de Silva	
			p280		Manuel de Mella	
			p282		Juan de Allón	
			p284		Luis Fernández Tristan, brother of Violante Rios (rel. est. 1649)	

No.	Year	Vol.	Pages	Document No.	Name of Accused or Document	Charge and Comments
494	1642	414	p286	4	Francisca Tinoco	Test. of Isabel Antúnez
			p288		Micaela Enríquez	
			p293		Catalina Enríquez	
			p299		Francisco Texoso	
			p302		Clara Texoso	
			p305		Isabel Texoso	
495	1642	414	p308	5	Isabel de Rivera	Test. of Antonio López
			p310		Esperanza Rodríguez	de Orduña
			p313		Margarita de Rivera	
			p316		Catalina Enríquez	
496	1642	414	p326	6	Simón Váez, Castello Blanco	Test. of Isabel de Granada
			p329		María de Rivera	Test. of Rafael de
			p337		Micaela Enríquez	Granada against
			p339		Gabriel de Granada	all except Simón
			p343		Pedro de Castro	Vaez, Castello
			p357		Margarita de Rivera	Blanco (Isabel de
			p363		Isabel de Rivera	Granada only
			p369		Blanca de Rivera	against Simón
			p374		Francisco López, el Chato	Vaez)
497	1642	414	p376	6a	Manuel Díaz, store-keeper	Test. of Pedro de Espinoza
			p378		Antonio Vaez Castelo Blanco	
			p380		María de Rivera	
			p383		Clara Rivera	
			p385		Isabel de Rivera	
			p387		Simón de Espinosa	
			p389		Francisco López Díaz, el Chato	
			p391		Isabel de Espinosa	
			p397		Violante Suárez	
			p402		Micaela Rodríguez	
			p404		Blanca Enríquez	
			p406		Clara de Silva (rel. est. 1649)	
498	1642	414	p410	7	Mathias Rodríguez de Olivera	Test. of Clara Enríquez
			p412		Ana Suárez (re-laxed 1648)	Test. of Pedro de Espinosa
			p414		Catalina de Rivera	
			p418		Rodrigo Serrano	
			p423		Gaspar Núñez	
499	1642	414	p437	8	Manuel Acosta	Test. of Simon Suárez de Espinosa
			p451		Justa Laponte	Test. of Tomás Núñez
			p452		Diego Méndez de Silva	de Peralta
			p453		María de Rivera	
			p457		Francisco López Díaz	
			p460		Simón Fernández	

No.	Year	Vol.	Pages	Document No.	Name of Accused or Document	Charge and Comments
			p465		Antonio Carvallo (b. Badajos, Spain)	
			p470		Antonio Váez Castelo Blanco	
			p473		Clara de Rivera	
			p476		Francisco de Texoso	
			p478		Antonio Vaez	
500	1642	414	p481	9	Blanca de Rivera	Test. of Elena de Silva
			p514		Leonor Vaez Rojas	
			p525		Simón Rodríguez Vaez or Arias	Test. of Juana Enríquez
			p531		Catalina Rivera (died before final sentence)	
			p534		Catalina Enríquez	
			p538		María de Rivera	
			p550		Antonio Vaéz Castelo Blanco	
501	1642	414	p555	10	Enrique de Miranda	Test. of Catalina Rivera
			p558		Manuel de Granada	Test. of Juana Enríquez
			p560		Micaela Enríquez	Test. of Beatriz Enríquez
			p565		Blanca Xuárez	
			p570		Isabel Enríquez (b. Málaga, Spain)	
			p583			Test. of Catalina Enríquez, the old woman
			p587		Antonio Carballo (merchant)	
			p591		Diego Antunez	
			p595		Gaspar Núñez	
			p599		Esperanza Jerónima, wife of Sebastina Roman; daughter of Juana Rodríguez, (r. *Puebla*)	
			p601		Diego de Figueroa	
502	1642	415	p1	1	Juan de Araujo	Test. of María de Rivera
			p2		Pedro López Monforte	
			p4		Julián de Albalaez	
			p12		Isabel de Segovia or Isabel de Campos	
			p27		Catalina de Rivera (rel. est. with her bones 1649)	
			p31		Antonio Rodríguez Núñez	
			p38		Miguel Núñez (de Guerto, alias Huerta; b. Cubillana; rel. est. 1649)	
			p41		Manuel de Mella	
			p47		Simón Fernández	
			p52		Duarte Rodríguez	
			pp55		Juana Rodríguez	

No.	Year	Vol.	Pages	Document No.	Name of Accused or Document	Charge and Comments
			p61		Juan Méndez	
			p63		Francisco de Campos, son of Alvaro Núñez de Segovia & Cridonia de Campos	
			p70		Micaela Enríquez	
			p76		Rafaela Enríquez	
			p83		Nuño de Silva	
			p86		Pedro de Castro	
			p89		Ana de Campos	
			p95		Gabriel Arias	
			p97		Diego Tinoco	
			p99		Alvara de Acuña (Port.; merchant; *dogmatista*)	
			p101		Juan de Ayllón (Port.; broker of Negroes in Catalina Pedroso)	
			p106		Manuel de Granada	
			p112		Jerónimo de Rojas, servant in mines of *Zacatecas*	
			p114		Diego Suárez de Figueroa	
			p118		Luis Pérez	
			p121		Gaspar Rodríguez de Segura	
			p124		Diego de Campos	
			p127		Melchor Rodríguez (de Huerta, alias Orta; rel. est 1649)	
			p130		Inés López	
			p133		Ana Enríquez	
			p139		Violante Suárez	
			p142		Francisca Núñez (rel. est. 1649)	
			p146		Catalina Maldonado	
			p149		Tomás López Monforte	
			p152		Sebastian Román (rel. est. 1649)	
			p157		Ana Tristán, alias Enríquez (b. Seville; daughter of Isabel Tristán)	
			p163		Beatriz Texoso (b. Lima, Peru; maiden; r. *Veracruz*)	
			p166		Gabriel Gómez Texoso	
			p172		Antonio Carvallo	
			p177		Clara Texoso	
			p180		Blanca Enríquez	
			p190		Fernándo Goyz Matos	
			p193		Nuño Pérez	
			p196		Francisco López, el Chato	
			p199		Diego Núñez	
			p202		Juan López de Guarda	

No.	Year	Vol.	Pages	Document No.	Name of Accused or Document	Charge and Comments
			p204		María Rodríguez	
			p208		Juan Tinoco	
			p222		Isabel de Rivera	
			p229		Antonio Vara, Castelo Blanco	
			p234		Catalina Enríquez	
			p241		Isabel Texoso	
			p244		Francisco Gómez de Medina the squint-eyed (el tuerto)	
			p247		Clara de Silva	
			p250		Simón Lucena	
			p254		Ana Enríquez	
			p256		Francisca Núñez (rel. est. 1649)	
			pp104,105, pp351-354 pp455-458		Manuel Díaz	
			pp155,6; pp290,1; pp453,4		Simón Espinosa	
			p92 et seq. p267 et seq.		Juan López Enríquez	
			p58 et seq. p470 et seq.		Jorge Montoya, brother of Francisco Dias Montoya,	
			p49		Rodríquez Falero Gaspar	
			p105		Manuel Rodríguez	
			p97		Diego Tinoco	
			p297		Juan Ramirez López	
503	1642	415	p264	2	María de Rivera	Test. Isabel Núñez
			p264		Justa Méndez	
			p267		Francisco López Enríquez, broker (rel. est. 1649)	
			p272		Isabel Enríquez	
			p276		Ana Enríquez	
			p280		Marcos Rodríguez Tristan	
			p282		Isabel Enríquez (r. *Puebla*)	
			p284		Gaspar Núñez	
			p288		Isabel de Rivera	
504	1642	415	p290	3	Simón Espinosa	Test. of Manuel Rodríguez Núñez
			p299		Tomé Gómez (rec. Apr. 1646) Lope Xuárez	Test. of Tomás Núñez de Peralta
			p301		Alvaro de Acuña	
			p303		Felipe de Burgos	
			p307		Antonio de Burgos	
			p310		Nuño de Silva	

No.	Year	Vol.	Pages	Document No.	Name of Accused or Document	Charge and Comments
			p312		Clara Texoso	
			p315		Blanca Suárez	
			p319		Gaspar de Alfaro	
			p323		Juan López de Guardia	
			p328		Pedro de Castro	
			p331		Jerónimo Núñez	
			p338		Catalina Enríquez	
			p344		Blanca Enríquez	
			p347		Manuel Diaz (a/k/a Manuel Diaz de Castella)	
			p353		Isabel de Espino	
			p355		Micaela Enríquez	
			p360		Antonio Rodríguez Arias (rel. est. 1649)	
505	1642	415	p362	4	Juan de Roxas	Test. of Isabel Antúnez
			p364		Juan Méndez	
			p366		López Núñez	
			p368		Beatriz de Alva	
			p370		Juan Duarte	
			p372		Manuel de Mella	
			p374		María Rodríguez	
			p378		Clara de Rivera	
			p380		Isabel de Espinosa	
			p383		Juan de Ayllon (rel. est. 1649)	
			p385		Alvaro Núñez de Segovia	
			p387		Isabel de Campos	
			p389		Alvaro de Acuña (died at sea)	
			p391		Blanca Méndez or de Rivera	
			p394		Blanca de Rivera	
			p398		Francisco de Matos	
			p400		López Xuárez	
			p402		Gómez de Silva	
			p404		Beatriz de Texoso (daughter of relajados; rel. est. 1649)	
			p407		María de Rivera	
			p410		Ana Enríquez	
			p412		Gaspar Rodríguez de Segura	
			p414		Isabel Núñez	
			p418		Francisco Núñez	
506	1642	415	p429	5	Luis de Mesquita	Test. of Violante Suárez
			p431		Roque Díaz Callero	
			p434		Blanca Enríquez	
			p437		María de Rivera	
			p441		Francisco Núñez	
			p444		Enrique Fernández	
			p446		Nuño de Figueroa (rec. 1646)	

No.	Year	Vol.	Pages	Document No.	Name of Accused or Document	Charge and Comments
			p448		Simón Fernández	
			p451		Manuel Alva	
			p453		Simón de Espinosa	
			p455		Manuel Díaz Santillan	
			p459		Simón López	
			p461		Tomás Treviño de Sobremonte	
			p463		Alvaro Núñez de Segovia	
			p465		Isabel de Espinosa	
			p467		Catalina Enríquez Tinoco	
			p470		Jorge de Montoya	
			p472		Isabel de Campos	
			p475		Gómez de Silva	
507	1642	415	p478	6	Manuel de Granada	Test. of Catalina
			p480		Miguel Núñez de Huerta	Enríquez de Silva
			p482		María de Vasquez	
			p484		Ana Vasquez	
			p487		Isabel Enríquez	
			p489		Gabriel Arias	
			p491		Diego Suárez de Figueroa	
			p497		Gaspar de Robles	
			p499		Blas López	
			p501		Manuel Díaz Santillana	
			p503		Manuel de Acosta	
			p506		Violante Suárez	
			p508		Manuel de Mella	
			p510		Nuño de Figueroa	
			p512		Jerónimo Esperanza	
			p514		Clara Enríquez	
			p516		Isabel de Medina	
			p518		Esperanza Rodríguez, mulato	
508	1642	415	p526	7	Antonio de Castro	Test. of Da. Isabel de
			p530		Pedro Fernández de Castro	Silva
			p533		Isabel de Campos	
			p544		Diego Tinoco	
			p547		Nuño de Silva Xuárez	
			p553		Isabel Méndez Huerta	
			p561		Esperanza Rodríguez	
			p564		Felipe López Noreña	
			p568		Juan Duarte	
			p573		Diego López Rivero, husband of Blanca Rivera (rel. est. 1649)	
			p577		Gaspar de Robles	
			p581		Juan González de Escobar	
			p584		Luis Núñez Pérez	
			p588		Isabel de Mella	
			p594		Medina, el Tuerto	
			p598		Diego Antonio	

No.	Year	Vol.	Pages	Document No.	Name of Accused or Document	Charge and Comments
			p602		Juan Rodríguez	
			p606		Francisco Texoso	
			p615		Jerónima Esperanza	
509	1643	416	5pp	1	Action by Attorney for Royal Treasurer against a Familiar of the Inquisition (Manuel Alvarez de Fuente) for a debt of 835 pesos that he owes to Juan Méndez de Villaviciosa— imprisoned for judaizante	
510	1642	416	p20 p63	Manila 2	Antonio Potello Simón Vaez de Sevilla	(2) in Manila his goods
511	1643	416	p182	7	a List of persons who testified but were not prisoners and depositions of those who saw, heard, treated, and communicated—and of people absent or dead in New Spain	
512	1643	416	p203	9	Tomás Núñez de Peralta	Test. of the Jew
513	1643	416	p209	11	Isabel de Rivera	Her testimony
514	1643	416	p227	14	Captain Domingo de Linares	(3) Inf. R. *Valladolid* [Now *Morelia*.] Also charged for working his slaves on holidays and saying there was no hell
515	1643	416	12pp	15	Don Francisco de Texoso	(2) His Dec.
516	1643	416	p293	24	Simón Vaez de Sevilla	Action about his goods
517	1643	416	p356	34	Andres Botello	(2) Accusation from Comisario in Phillipines
518	164-	416	p412	37	Edict of S. O. that all those who had property of Jews in their possession should denounce them Antonio Díaz Estremos Order of imprisonment Jorge de Montoya Francisca Díaz Montoya	
519	1643-	416	pp427, 466-468	38	Melchor Juárez, secretary of Bishop Palafox. Helpful to Jews in the Inquisition. (This entry is a draft of letters sent to Supreme Council and covers years below	
			p430		Diego Ximenez de la Cámara	(2) 1643, 1646, 1647, 1650, 1653-1656. Some letters are
			p438		Marques de Villena	(2) without date and
			pp434,466		Don Guillen de Lamprat	(2) some seem to be from 1641 to 1644
			p440		Francisco de Rojas Ayaro	(2)
			p438		a Palafox	(2)

No.	Year	Vol.	Pages	Document No.	Name of Accused or Document	Charge and Comments
			p442		The Rivera family	(2)
					Gaspar de Robles	(2)
520	1642	416	p530	41	Jorge Espinoza	Letter to Supreme
					Juan Pacheco de León	Council giving re-
					Luis Núñez Pérez	port on cases
					Pedro Espinoza	
					Sebastían Cardoso,	
					son of Diego Cardoso	
					Aseitero and Antonia	
					Gómez	
					Dn. Jorge Orozco	
			p501	40	Antonio de Peralta	Relaxed previously
521	1649	416	p536	42	a Letters to Supreme Council concerning those	
					who were to receive sambenitos, of the autos-	
			p539		de-Fe (pp538-544) and Juan Pacheco de León	
522	1643	416	p567	43	Memorandum of prisoners who had given tes-	
					timony and who were exiled to Spain where	
					they were condemned—(Signs of the Jews)	
523	1643	417		14	Antonio Caraballo	Test. of Nuño de
						Figueroa
			p455		Diego Núñez	Test. of Manuel Acosta
					Francisco Acosta	They lived in Puebla
524	1643	417		16	Manuel Acosta	Test., his
					Christobal Rodríguez	Test., his, for solici-
					Méndez	tation
			p468		Diego Núñez	Test. of Isabel Antúnez
			p470		Diego Osorio	Test. of Hernándo de
						la Peña
			p471		Cristobal de Lugo	Test. of Hernándo de
						la Peña
			p474		Blanca de Rivera	Her Test.
			p482		Isabel de Texoso	Test. of Francisco
						Texoso
			p505		Clara de Texoso	Test. of Francisco
						Texoso
			p522		Catalina de Rivera	Test. of Francisco
						Texoso
			p523		Clara de Rivera	Test. of Francisco
						Texoso
			p527		María de Rivera	Test. of Francisco
						Texoso
			p528		Gómez de Silva	Test. of Francisco
						Texoso
			p536		Elena or Isabel de	Test. of Agustina de
					Silva	Carera
					Leonor de Rojas	Test. of Agustina de
						Carera
					Antonio Vaez	Test. of Agustina de
					Castelo Blanco	Carera
					Simón Vaez de	Test. of Agustina de
					Sevilla	Carera
					Antonio Carballo	Test. of Agustina de
						Carera

No.	Year	Vol.	Pages	Document No.	Name of Accused or Document	Charge and Comments
			p537		Justa Méndez	Test. of Felipa de la Cruz
			p539		Marcos de Useta	Test. of Juan de Caba
					Luis Becerra	Test. of Gertrudis Villanueva
			p542		Felipa, wife of Lic. Tabasco	Test. of María Bautista
					Beatriz Enríquez	Test. of María Bautista
					Micaela Enríquez	Test. of María Bautista
					Miguel Tinoco	Test. of María Bautista
			p545		Isabel de Espinosa	Test. of Rafael Silva
			p549		Manuel Alvarez de Arellano	Test. of Gaspar Gutíerrez
525	1643	417	p554 p558	18	Luis de Mezquita	Test. of Pedro de León, Catalina González, and Magdalena González
			p560		Gaspar Alfaro	
			p562		Simón de Espinosa	Test. of María de la Cruz
					Juana Tinoco	
			p563		Gerónimo Rojas	Test. of Sebastián Díaz
			p565		Catalina de Espinosa	Test. of Francisco Fernández
			p567		Antonio de García	Simón Alvarez
					The Blancas	
					Rafaela Enríquez	
					Francisco Díaz (Port.)	
526	1643	417	p582	20	Da. Agustina de Luna y Arellano	Capt. Tomás de Suosnabar y Aguirre, Chief Constable S. O.
527	1643	418	300pp	1	Manuel de Acosta, a/k/a Francisco de Torres	(7) Pro., b. Lisbon
528	1643	418	p405	6	Tomás López Monforte (b. Monfort, Port.; rec. 1646)	(2) Case. Port. (son of Francisco Gómez, merchant and Costanza López)
529	1643	418	p457	7	Domingo Flores	(7) Pro., r. *Tlaxcala*
530	1643	418	p486	10	Isabel Enríquez	(2) Test. of Da. Micaela Enríquez
					Ramón López Ramírez	
					Blas López	
					Alvaro de Acuña	(2) Test. of Da. Blanca Suárez
					Beatriz Rodríguez Alva	
					Alvaro Núñez (de Segovia—rel. est. 1649)	
					Blas López	
531	1644	419	pp3-19	2	a Report of Treasury concerning sequestered property of prisoners and some vouchers of payment	

No.	Year	Vol.	Pages	Document No.	Name of Accused or Document	Charge and Comments
532	1644	419	p39	4	Alvaro de Acuña	(2) Test. (rel. est. 1649)
533	1644	419	pp57-132	6	Esperanza Rodríguez, mulato (rec. with sambenito 1646)	(2) Acts in her case
534	1644	419	p203	15	Felipe Burgos	(2) Test., Port.
535	1644	419	p208-211	16	Catalina Enríquez (relaxed in person 1649)	(2) Test. also at pp311-321, 343-499, 506-527, 553-558, 578-584, 591
536	1644	419	p212	17	Gonzálo Rodríguez	(2) Test.
537	1644	419	p217	18	Ruy Fernández Pereyra	(2) Test.
538	1644	419	p222	a	Letter from Inq. of Seville accompanied by list of persons who testified there	
539	1644	419	p241	23	Fernándo Andrade	(2) Test.
540	1644	419	p252	25	Diego Núñez	(2) Test.
541	1644	419	p265	27	Fernándo de Mezquita	(2) Test.
542	1644	419	p269	28	D. Mayor Alvarez	(2) Test.
543	1644	419	p273	29	Marcos Rodríguez Tristán	(2) Test.
544	1644	419	p280	30	Enrique Méndez	(2) Test.
545	1644	419	p288	32	Dr. Simón Núñez and other persons	(2) Test. of Catalina Enríquez and Simón Montero
546	1644	419	p310	33	Copy of a letter written by Francisco López to his brother Simón Vaez of Seville (judaizantes)	
547	1644	419	p321	34	Francisco López Correa	(2) Test.
548	1644	419	p328	35	Leonor Núñez	(2) Test.
549	1644	419	p334	36	Antonio de Burgos	(2) Test.
550	1644	419	p344	37	Gerónimo Fernández Correa	(2) Test. (rec. Jan. 23, 1647)
551	1644	419	p351	38	Blanca Enríquez	(2) Test., also pp405-408
552	1644	419	p361	39	Clara Enríquez	(2) Test.
553	1644	419	p374	40	Fernándo Rodríguez (rec. 1647)	(2) Test., also pp507-513
554	1644	419	p396	41	Rodrigo Fernández Bachiller	(2) Test.
555	1644	419	p409	42	Francisco Sánchez de Sosa	(2) Test.

No.	Year	Vol.	Pages	Document No.	Name of Accused or Document	Charge and Comments
556	1644	419	p413	43	Francisco de Medina	(2) Test.
557	1644	419	p416	44	Laureana Méndez	(2) Test.
558	1644	419	p421	45	Isabel Correa	(2) Test.
559	1644	419	p425	46	Ana Correa	(2) Test.
560	1644	419	p452	51	Manuel Enríquez	(2) Test.
561	1644	419	p475	56	Francisco Rodríguez	(2) Test.
562	1644	419	p482	57	Jorge Rodríguez Tavares	(2) Test.
563	1644	419	p513	59	Rodrigo Fernández	(2) Test.
564	1644	419	p553	62	Against *other Jews*	(2) Test. of Juan Cardoso
565	1644	419	p579	63	Miguel López Correa	(2) Test.
566	1648	421	p201	6	Bernardo López de Mendizabal	(2) And other crimes. Accusation
567	1648	421	p306	8	Leonor de Agurto Duarte Rodríguez Juan Méndez	Test. of Antonio Fernández Chillón Test. of Juan Cardoso
568	1645	421		10	Draft of letter from S. O. to Inq. General containing incomplete list of acts about Simón Vaez and others whose religion is not stated	
569	1645	421	pp333-452	11	Juan Cardoso Antonio Méndez Chillón Clara Méndez Margarita de Rivera Leonor Enríquez Antonio Xuárez Clara Texoso Pedro Jorge (who fought with Dutch against the Spaniards)	Test. Test. (Rec. 1647) Test. Test.
570	1645	421	p512	22	Melchor Rodríguez Manuel de Huerta Manuel López	Incomplete Test.
571	1646	423	p1	*Campeche* 1	Diego López Coson, alias Diego López Núñez, son of Leonor Núñez	(2) Pro.
572	1646	423	p38	2	Juan de Morales	(2) Pro.
573	1642		p440	3	Antonio Rodríguez Arias	Test. of María Rivera in which there are several edicts
574	1646	425	p464	*San Luis Potosi* 5	María de Aguilar Pablo de Sola Francisco López Lobo	(4) Test. of Antonio Arismena Gogorrón. All three are Port.

No.	Year	Vol.	Pages	Document No.	Name of Accused or Document	Charge and Comments
575	1646	425	p471	6	Francisco de Fonseca Pedro Rodríguez Matos, a/k/a "Los Reyes"	(2) Pro. with denunciation of the accused against other person in this entry and himself
576	1642	425	p521	12	Luis Gómez Lobo	Test. of María de Rivera
					Francisco Campos Lope de Mezquita, alias Amezquita Juan Rodríguez Xuárez	Test. of Bartolomé Alfaro
			p531		Gaspar Rodríguez de Segura	
			p535		Beatriz López	
			p553		Sánchez de Sosa	Test. of Francisco López Correa
			p540		Isabel Enríquez	Test. of Micaela Enríquez
					Juan de Lurriaga	Test. of Francisco Arévalo
577	1646	426	p411	7	Blanca de Ribera and *other people*	(2) Test.
578	1646	426	p412		Luis Núñez Perez & *others*	(2) Test.
579	1646	426	p412		Da. Catalina Enríquez	(2) Test. against her and her Test. against others
580	1646	426	p413		Against other Jews	(2) Test. of Catalina de Rivera
581	1646	426	p414		Against other Jews	(2) Test. of Manuel Carrasco
582	1646	426	p414		Against other Jews	(2) Test. of Esperanza Rodríguez
583	1646	426			Other Jews	Test. of Gaspar Vaez
584	1646	426	p417		Other Jews	Test. of Rafaela Enríquez
585	1646	426	p418		Testimony sent to Spain in the year 1648 concerning Sebastián Cardoso and his entire case up to Inq. punishment. (rec. 1648)	
586	1646	426	pp491- 499		Votes of the Inq. concerning the Auto de fe of 1646	
587	1641	426	pp500- 506		Autos de fe of April 16, 1646; Jan. 23, 1647 (see p507)	
588	1646	426	p516		Duarte de León Xaramillo	Publication of Test.
589	1646	426	p519		Leonor Núñez	(2) Publication of Test.
590	1646	426	p520		María Gómez	(2) Publication of Test.

No.	Year	Vol.	Pages	Document No.	Name of Accused or Document	Charge and Comments
591	1646	426	p521		Francisco López Blandon	(2) Publication of Test.
592	1646	426	p522		Tomás Tremiño de Sobremonte	(2) Publication of Test.
593	1646	426	p523		Antonia Núñez, daughter of Duarte de León	(2) Publication of Test.
594	1646	426	p524		Simón de León, son of Duarte de León	(2) Publication of Test.
595	1646	426	p524 Vta.		Ana Núñez (13 years old), daughter of Duarte de León	(2) Publication of Test.
596	1646	426	p525		Francisco de León, son of Duarte de León	(2) Publication of Test.
597	1646	426	p525		Simón Montero	(2) Publication of Test.
598	1646	426	p527		Simón Montero	(2) Publication of Test.
599	1646	426	p528 Vta.		Simón López de Aguarda	(2) Publication of Test.
600	1646	426	p529		Juan Duarte	Publication of Test.
601	1646	426	p530		Jorge de León	(2) Publication of Test.
602	1646	426	p531		Francisco Luis	(2) Publication of Test.
603	1646	426	p532		Fernándo de Goys y Matos	(2) Publication of Test.
604	1646	427	52pp	2	Papers about Manuel Carrasco, rec. *auto* April 16, 1646, and inventory of his sugar plantation and machinery	
605		427	38pp	4	Action by S. O. against *Da. Andrea de Villaloba,* wife of Antonio Fuentes, for $166 which she owed for the house of *Diego Rodríguez Arias* (who had been rec. and his property confiscated) his mother was Da. Blanca Enríquez rel. est. with her husband Antonio Rodríguez Arias - April 11, 1649	
606	1646	427	3pp	5	Test. about the sale of a mulato child called Diego Arias for $195, by Diego Rodríguez Arias	
607	1646	427	8pp	6	Esperanza Rodríguez Juana del Bosque Isabel and María del Bosque	Hearing before the Treasury concerning the property of the people rec.
608	1648	427	7pp	10	Diego Rodríguez Arias	Hearing before Treasury
609	1648	427	23pp	*Guadalajara* 14	Juan Duarte de Espinosa	Suit against him by S. O. for $200
610	1647	429	p284	5	Antonio de Rojas	Papers found on him when imprisoned

No.	Year	Vol.	Pages	Document No.	Name of Accused or Document	Charge and Comments
611	1647	429	p392 p391	13	Rivero, ironworker Catalina de Campos	(4) Den. Port. (4) Den.
612	1648	430	pp48-540	*Campeche*	Pedro de Campos	(1,2) Pro., tortured
613	1648	430	p560	7	Vaez de Acevedo	(2) Pro. C. C.; letters from Phillipines
614	1648	431	p71	*Chamacue-ro* 3	Juan de Alvarez or Alvalez	(2) Pro. & Test. Fugitive
615	1648	431	p96	4	Jorge Duarte	(2) Test. and Pro.
616	1648	431	p80	*Mixquia-hua*	Antonio Baez Castelo Blanco	S. O. order to seques-ter property
617	1649	431	p510		Isabel de Campos	(2) Pro.
618	1649	431	p559		Gonzálo Díaz (rel. est. 1649)	(2) Pro.
619	1649	432	p46	7 a	Acts against some rec. people who made a pretext of going to Veracruz to embark for Spain but remained in *Puebla*	
620	1649	433	p492		Pedro Arías Maldonado (dec'd)	(2) Pro. (merchant; *Veracruz;* rel. est.)
621	1649	433	p538		Pedro de Torres	(2) Pro.
622	1649	434	p26		Action by Royal Treasurer against Fernán Gómez for $37 which he owes to Antonio Rodríguez Arias, whose property had been confiscated by S. O.	
623	1654	434	p216		Action by Royal Treasurer against the prop-erty of Juan Duarte de Espinosa	
624	1655	434	p250		Elena de Silva (Baez) Isabel de Silva Gómez de Silva Antonio Carballo, married to Isabel Silva, alias Correa (rec. 1649)	Account taken of all the goods deposited by the accuseds
625	1690	435	p3	1	Antonio Pérez (Port.)	Test. against him (a laborer) for saying that Tremiño (who died at stake) had been a good Jew for dying in his Law
626	1690	435	p11	4	Francisco Luis	Pro., because he de-nied that there was sufficient grounds for the punishment imposed upon him in 1649
627	1690	435	p12	5	Diego Pérez de Villadiego	(4) Pro. No. 1

No.	Year	Vol.	Pages	Document No.	Name of Accused or Document	Charge and Comments
628	1690	435	p15	8	Pedro González	(4) Pro.
629	1690	435	p22	13	Guillermo Enríquez	A foreigner, for wearing silk after Inq. had ordered him to wear sambenito
630	1650	435	p76-80, p86-88	30	Pedro Alvarez	(2) Den., r. *San Miguel*
631	1650	435	p95	*Toluca* 35	Ana del Valle	Den. for having heard her mother say that María Gómez, her cousin, had been relaxed without having been a relapso
632	1650	435	p95	36	Isabel, niece of Marcos del Valle	(4) Den., r. in *Toluca*
633	1650	435	p95	*Toluca* 37	Violante Méndez	Den. for having said that her sister, Ana Gómez, had been relaxed without having been a relapso
634	1650	435	p96	*Toluca*	Jerónimo del Valle, rec. for judaizante	Den. because leaving school he jumped over and spit on a cross on the floor
635	1650	435	p137	*Veracruz* 100	Gaspar Andres	Den. for saying that the leg of an animal had not been well roasted because the landrecilla had not been removed
636	1650	435	p137	*Veracruz*	Antonio Gonzáles Jamaica	(4) Den. and same statement as previous case
637	1650	435	p165	*San Luis de la Paz*	Luis de Tobar y Torres	(4) Den. and irreverence in church
638	1650	435	p182		Luis de Tovar	For being of the Jewish race
639	1650	435	p244	*Oaxtepec*	Isabel de Alba	For wearing silk, being the daughter and sister of penitents of the Inq.
640	1650	435	p254	*Cuautla*	Francisco de Herrera	Test.; for suspicion of locking himself up with his son to perform Jewish rites or to commit nefarious sins

No.	Year	Vol.	Pages	Document No.	Name of Accused or Document	Charge and Comments
641	1650	435	p265	*Oaxtepeque*	Antonio de Herrera	Den. for having closed himself with his father (previous entry) for same purposes
642	1650	435	p265	*Oaxtepeque*	Antonio Pérez	Den. for statements about Sebastian Vaez de Acevedo (1), who had been imprisoned
643	1650	435	p322	*Cholula*	María Marin & siblings	Den. for using silk, arms, and a horse; being grandchildren of penitents and those whose bones had been burned by the S. O.
644	1650	435	p338	*Cholula*	Diego Ruiz	Den. for being a descendant of Jews
645	1650	435	p339		Pro. against Jewish penitents in *Puebla* for walking at night, the men in full dress and the women likewise, and with mantillas	
646	1650	435	p388	*Veracruz*	José de Campos	Den. for saying that he could not believe that his uncle, Francisco de Campos, had been a Jew
647	1650	435	p388		Manuel Barbosa	Den. for having communication with people descended from Jews
648	1650	435	p404		Francisco Díaz de Montoya (rec. for judaizante)	For saying that God knew that he had been and was a Christian
649	1650	435	p404		Sebastian Baez de Acevedo, penitent with sambenito with a cross, etc.	Den. for saying that he had been a Christian and that there had been false testimony
650	1690	435	p5		Francisco de Sosa	Pro., for saying that Indians had to have been punished with Tremiño, relaxed secretly
651	1690	435	pp41,44,45		Francisco Blandon	(4) Pro.
652	1690	435	pp32,41,54		Juan, mulato, from district of *Villa de Lagos*	Pro., about Jewish rites

No.	Year	Vol.	Pages	Document No.	Name of Accused or Document	Charge and Comments
653	1650	436	pp42, 52,58		Gaspar de Viveros	(2) Test.
654	1650	436	p61	*Temascat-lepec*	Alonso García de Rivero (6 years of age, son of a Port.)	(4) Inf., he said that he saw in Christ "a faith that was not good in that place"
655	1650	436	p81	16	Juan Rivero	(2) Test.
656	1653	437	p418	a	Diego Pita Anunciba (Port.)	For saying that some penitents of the auto de fe had been unjustly convicted

Tomo 5 (214 pages) covering Volumes 438 to 560.

No.	Year	Vol.	Pages	Document No.	Name of Accused or Document	Charge and Comments
657	1679	438	1p	*Michoacán* 41	Canon Juan O. de Garay is informed that D. Mateo de Cisneros, Vicar General (an ecclesiastical judge) of *Michoacán,* his parents and ancestors, are citizens of Toledo, Jews, and that they had sambenitos in the Church of San Vicente	
658	1662	439	35pp	22	Ana de la Peña Juan Márquez	(3) r. *Tepeaca* (3) r. *Tepeaca*
659	1662	439	84pp	24	Capt. Matias Pereyra Lobo	(3) Cause
660	1652	441	5pp	3	Gayan, a family of criminal penitents	Acts and notification to comply with exile
661	1656	441	7pp	4	Simón Suárez de Espinoza Juan Tinoco & wife	Act about the departure & compliance with banishment
662	1659	446	p220	*Ecatepec* 7	Juan Bello	(2) Test., also cruelty to slaves
663	1663	447	p372		Juan Duarte Espinoza (rec.)	Edicts and acts of creditors against his property
664	1681	450	18pp	*Querétaro* 10	Gabriel de Arellano, alias "the hairless"	(1) Instituted by the Fiscal of the S. O.
665	1602	452	p14		Francisco Rodríguez, barber	Test. because his son said that he had worn sambenito
666	1602	452	p26	8	Mariana de Mirabel	Test. because she removed the landrecilla from the leg of the sheep
667	1602	452	p136	*Los Reyes*	Cristobal Gómez, (rel.)	Test. about his death and hacienda

No.	Year	Vol.	Pages	Document No.	Name of Accused or Document	Charge and Comments
668	1602	452	p207		Juan Fernández	Test., a son of rec. was wearing silk
669	1602	452	p207		Arellano	Test. [same as previous entry]
670	1602	452	p215	*Puebla*	Gerónimo Rodríguez	(3) Test. Previously penanced by S. O.
671	1602	452	p278	*Puebla*	Diego de Madrigal	Test. He always swore by the God of Israel
672	1602	452	p292		Andres Pacheco	(3) Test.
673	1602	452	p330	*Acapulco*	Luis de Peñaloes	(3) Test.
674	1642	453	p1		Isabel Campos	(2) Test. against her
675	1642	453	p6		Clara Antúnez	(2) Test. against her
676	1642	453	p11-31, 475,476		Clara de Rivera	(2) Test. against her
677	1642	453	p32		Diego Antúnez	(2) Test. against him
678	1642	453	p34		Rafael Gómez Cardoso	(2) Test. against him
679	1642	453	p39		Antonio Gómez Carballo	(2) Test. against him
680	1642	453	p44		Antonio Rodríguez Núñez	(2) Test. against him
681	1642	453	p46		Miguel Núñez de Huerta	(2) Test. against him
682	1642	453	p49		Antonio Baez Castelo Blanco	(2) Test. against him
683	1642	453	p54		Diego Mendoza de Silva	(2) Test. against him
684	1642	453	p56		María Rodríguez	(2) Test. against her
685	1642	453	p59		Luis Núñez Pérez	(2) Test. against him
686	1642	453	p85		Simón Fernández (rec. 1647)	(2) Test. against him
687	1642	453	p65		Francisco López Díaz	(2) Test. against him
688	1642	453	p71		Francisco Texoso	(2) Test. against him
689	1642	453	p76		Da. Ana Tristán	(2) Test. against her
690	1642	453	p79		Da. Blanca Enríquez	(2) Test. against her
691	1642	453	p91		Diego Núñez	(2) Test. against him
692	1642	453	p94		Gaspar de Robles	(2) Test. against him
693	1642	453	p99		Violante Rodríguez (rel. est. 1649)	(2) Test. against him
694	1642	453	p102		Violante Xuárez	(2) Test. against him
695	1642	453	p107		Jerónimo Núñez	(2) Test. against him

No.	Year	Vol.	Pages	Document No.	Name of Accused or Document	Charge and Comments
696	1642	453	p110		Diego Tinoco	(2) Test. against him
697	1642	453	p115		Simón Montes	(2) Test. against him
698	1642	453	p126		María Baptista	(2) Test. against her
699	1642	453	p129		Duarte de Leon Xaramilla	(2) Test. against him (55 years old; twice previously in S. O.)
700	1642	453	p141		Clara de Silva	(2) Test. against her
701	1642	453	p150		Manuel de Mella	(2) Test. against him
702	1642	453	p336		Rafaela Enríquez	(2) Test. against her
703	1642	453	pp151-470, 533, etc.		Margarita de Rivera	Test. against her
704	1642	453	p363		Balnza Xuárez	(2) Test. against her
705	1642	453	p374		Clara Texoso	(2) Test. against her
706	1642	453	p381		Isabel Texoso	(2) Test. against her
707	1642	453	p388		Violante Tejoso	(2) Test. against her
708	1642	453	p393		Duarte Rodríguez Tejoso	(2) Test. against him
709	1642	453	p397		Francisco Tejoso	(2) Test. against him
710	1642	453	pp404-408, 464-470		Simón de Espinosa	(2) Test. against him
711	1642	453	p409		Alvaro de Acuña	(2) Test. against him
712	1642	453	p413		Justa Mendoza	(2) Test. against her
713	1642	453	p430		Micaela Enríquez	(2) Test. against her
714	1642	453	p448		Gaspar de Segura	(2) Test. against him
715	1642	453	p452		Isabel de Silva	(2) Test. against her
716	1642	453	p464		Blanca Enríquez	(2) Test. against her
717	1642	453	pp467,468 521-565		Da. María de Rivera	(2) Test. against her
718	1642	453	p471		Isabel de Granada	(2) Test. against her
719	1642	453	p477		Francisco de Aranz	(2) Test. against him
720	1642	453	p481		Isabel de Rivera	(2) Test. against her
721	1642	453	p483		Manuel Acosta	(2) Test. against him
722	1642	453	p485		Isabel de Francis	(2) Test. against her
723	1642	453	p487		María de Francis	(2) Test. against her
724	1642	453	p489		Catalina de Silva	(2) Test. against her
725	1642	453	p491		José Vasquez	(2) Test. against him
726	1642	453	p525		Catalina de Rivera	(2) Test. against her
727	1643	453	p528		Isabel Tinoco	(2) Test. against her
728	1632	453	p531		Blanca de Rivera	(2) Test. against her

No.	Year	Vol.	Pages	Document No.	Name of Accused or Document	Charge and Comments
729	1642	453	p562		Clara de Rivera	(2) Test. against her
730	1643	453	p568		Luis de Mezquita	(2) Test. against him (rec. 1646)
731	1643	453	p570		Nuño de Pérez	(2) Test. against him
732	1642	453	p573		Manuel de Segovia	(2) Test. against him
733	1642	453	p606		Francisco de Medina, the squint-eyed	(2) Test. against him
734	1642	453	p612		Manuel Alvarez Arellano	(2) Test. against him
735	1650	454	21pp	15 a	Alphabetical list of testimony sent in 1650 to the Inquisition in Cartagena gleaned from the procesos, votes, and prisoners of the autos de fe which had been celebrated. The prisoners were accomplices of Jewish practitioners	
736	1650	454	2pp	*Tlaxcala* 17	*Fulano* Seguera	Grandson of a relaxed
737	1650	454	2pp	*Tlaxacapa* 18	Pedro González	He didn't want to eat the meat of a suckling pig
738	1650	454	5pp	28 a	Documents exchanged between Viceroy Count of Alba and the S. O. about the exiled prisoners	
739	1650	454	10pp	29 a	The sending to Spain of the prisoners penanced by this Inq. and the receipt given by the General of the Navy who received them	
740	1612	455	p196	*Cuautla*	Leonor de Ordaz	(4) Inf., also witchcraft
741	1612	455	p287	*Acapulco*	Da. María de Reza	(4) (Judaizano) Test.
742	1612	455	p356	*Antequera*	The Pereira bakers	(5) Sons of penanced
743	1612	455	p606	*Antequera*	Xines de Herrero Osta (lawyer of San Luis Potosí)	For using silk and an entourage of Negroes, being the son of a woman burned at the stake in Spain, having confessed
744	1612	455	p805		Ana María and Francisco Calvo, clergyman	(4) Inf.
745	1612	455	p805		Francisco Calvo, clergyman	(4) Inf. filed by the captain of the boat which was almost shipwrecked
746	1654	457	p80	*Santa Maria de Parras*	Marta de San Joseph	She removed the landrecilla from the leg of the sheep

No.	Year	Vol.	Pages	Document No.	Name of Accused or Document	Charge and Comments
747	1660	460		Whole Volume	Domingo Marquez, Chief Constable of *Tepeaca,* also charged with grave crimes against the Catholic faith	(2) Pro. In the volume there is a letter written on a piece of linen
748	1644	463	p266		Beatriz Enríquez	(2) Test. against her
749	1642	463	p270		Isabel Antúnez & other Jews	(2) Test. against them
750	1642	464	p174		Juan Campos	(2) Test. against him
751	1706	465	580pp		Fr. Joseph de San Ignacio, alias Joseph Ignacio, also Juan Fernández de León	(2) And heresy, apostasy and bigamy. Expelled from Order of Bethlemites
752	1601	467	p15	6	Diego Pereyra	(4) Test., r. *Puebla*
753	1607	467	p102	27	Diego Correa (Port.)	(4) Test. from Prov. of Avalos
754	1607	467	p123	31 a	Juan Saravia	He called Antonio Castro, Port., "Jew dog"; r. *Minas de Escamela*
755	1607	467	p354		Juan Bautista, carpenter	(3) Test. & for saying that he lived in *Tetuán* for 4 years and was very happy with the Jews
756	1606	471	3pp	*Puebla* 11	Juan Bautista	Den. made by González
757	1606	471		28	Pedro Franco	For saying that he removed the landrecilla from the leg of the sheep
758	1606	471	3pp	51	"Fulano" Noguera	(3)
759	1606	471	2pp	61	Felipe Hernández, shoemaker	(1) Prior to arrest he fled
760	1606	471	9pp	*Puebla* 125	Fray Juan de Villegas teacher of the novices at San Agustin de la Puebla	Suspected of being an observer of the Law of Moses
761	1610	473	p199		Juan López	(4) Test.
762	1610	473	p248		Bartolomé Fernán (Flemish)	(4) Test.
763	1610	474	p333	*Guatemala*	Gaspar Pereira Cardoso	(2) Test.
764	1610	475	p712	*Amilpas* 25	María Suárez Carbajal	Test. for having said that while God would be God, the land would be His (or hers) in spite of Jewish knaves

No.	Year	Vol.	Pages	Document No.	Name of Accused or Document	Charge and Comments
765	1610	475	p746	27	a Francisco Cornejo	Suspected of not being a Christian
766	1644	477	p135		Francisco Texoso	(2) Dec.
767	1661	477	p153	13	Isabel and Ana, daughter and niece of Marcos del Valle	Test. against them; r. near *Toluca*
768	1610	478	p96	8	Alvaro Silvera	For using silk, being the son of one burned at stake
769	1613	478	p415	*Guardiana*	Francisco Paduano, Corsican	Using Jewish ceremonies
770	1642	483	p381		Da. Micaela Enríquez	(2) Test.
771	1618	485			a Prophecy in Hebrew found in a little marble box sent by the Papal Envoy to France to Cardinal Burgence	
772	1663	485	81pp		Beatriz Rodríguez or Vasquez, alias Unitas (She called herself Beatriz Buttz)	Pro. C. C.
773	1614	486	p68	*Guadala- jara*	Cristobal Herrera	(3)
774	1642	487	192pp	14	Luis Pérez Roldán	(7) Pro., C. C., b. Mexico City
775	1642	487	20pp	15	Diego Rodríguez	(2) Pro., C. C.
776	1642	487	102pp	18	Da. Blanca Suárez	(7) Pro., C. C.
777	1642	487	25pp	20	Clara de Rivera & daughter	For superstitions
778	1642	487	214pp	21	Da. Isabel Duarte or Antúnez	(7) Second part of proceso & C. C.
779	1625	488	247pp	5	Simón Bave Sevilla & Da. Juana Enríquez, his wife	(3) Pro., C. C. (Correct spelling should be Baez or Vaez)
780	1651	489	p127		Letter from Viceroy about the sending of Jews to Spain	
781	1649	489	p189		Antonio Baez alias Capt. Castelo Blanco	(2) C. C. Relaxed. Had been rec. in 1623
782	1642	492	87pp	3	Agustín Núñez de Rojas, *et al.*	Acts about their property
	1643	492	69pp	6	Proceeding by the Fiscal of the S. O. to recover $138 from Agustín Núñez de Rojas which belonged to the property of Simón Vaez Sevilla	
783	1642	492	66pp	*Guadala- jara* 5	a Francisco Núñez Navarro	Reports on their sequestered property
784	1639	495	12pp	*Vallado- lid* 14	Duarte de León	Den. by Francisco Enríquez de Silva

No.	Year	Vol.	Pages	Document No.	Name of Accused or Document	Charge and Comments
785	1647	497	66pp	*Veracruz* 8	Duarte de Castaño (Port.)	(7) Pro., C. C.; b. Abrantes
786	1642	498	5pp	1	Pedro de Espinosa	(2) Test. of Tomás Núñez de Peralta
787	1642	498	24pp	2	Juan Duarte	(2) Test. of Tomás Núñez de Peralta
					Gaspar de Robles	(2) Test. of Tomás Núñez de Peralta
788	1642	498	13pp	4	Juliana (Negress), Angola slave of Da. María de Ribera, Jewess	For not wanting to disclose what she knew of her mistress, mother, and sisters about observing the Law of Moses
789	1642	499	123pp		Luis de Amezquita	(2) Pro., b. in Segovia
790	1642	499	p124		Antonio de Robles	(2) Test.
791	1642	499	p130		Blanca Rodríguez	(2) Test.
792	1642	499	pp194-506		Antonio López de Orduña	(2) Pro., b. in Seville
793	1642	499	p517		Francisco Montoya Juan Tinoco María Rivera	The title of the preliminary procesos are ready to be added to the testimony against them by other prisoners
794	1642	499	pp520-663	9	Juana Rodríguez del Bosque	(2) Pro.
795	1642	500	14pp	2	Divers persons accused of (7)	(7) By Isabel de Silva
796	1642	500	28pp	8	Francisca Núñez	(7) Pro., C. C.
797	1642	500	109pp	5	Isabel Duarte or Antunez	(7) Pro., b. Seville; C. C.
798	1642	500	279pp	6	Blanca Méndez de Rivera	(2) Pro., C. C.
799	1642	501	25pp	22	Francisco Suarez de Aguilar	Resident of *Tepeaca*
800	1663	502		18	Acts and order for publication of the Edict of Faith in *Mixteca* because of the presumption that Port. Jews were there	
801	1649	503	19pp	4	Francisco de Campos Segobia (rel. est. 1649)	(2) Pro., C. C., Port.; died in *Veracruz*
802	1649	503	3pp	5	Cristobal de Acosta	(2) Pro., C. C.
803	1649	503	2pp	6	Enrique de Leon	(2) Pro., C. C.

No.	Year	Vol.	Pages	Document No.	Name of Accused or Document	Charge and Comments
804	1694	503	14pp	7	Antonio Narvaez, alias David Machorro	(2) Pro., C. C.
805	1649	503	2pp	*Puebla* 8	Juan García del Brocel	(2) Pro., C. C., r. *Los Angeles*
806	1649	503	2pp	9	Fernando Amezquite	(2) Pro., C. C.
807	1649	503	3pp	10	Benito Enríquez	(2) Pro., C. C.
808	1649	503	17pp	11	Pedro Texoso, father of the Texosos	(2) Pro. C. C.
809	1649	503	2pp	12	Gaspar de Segura	(2) Pro., C. C.
810	1649	503	pp26,27 66	a	Letter of the S. O. about the auto general de fe	
811	1649	503	2pp	34	Simón Fernández	(7) Test. of Beatriz Enríquez against him
812	1649	503		54	Action on the petition of the Officials of the S. O. about the expenses of $316 incurred on the repairing of the houses of Simón Vaez	
813	1649	503	8pp	55	Action by the Comisario of the S. O. (Campeche) against Gómez de Silva Elena de Silva, his wife	(These two penanced by the Inq. of Mexico.)
814	1649	503	81pp	*Los Angeles* 70	Jorge Jacinto Bazan Miguel Tinoco	(Head of the Pro. against these 2 penanced by the S. O.)
815	1650	504	26pp	*Tepozotlán* 3	Tomás López, dec'd, (Port.)	(7) Pro. C. C. (r. *Tepozotlán*) against his memory
816	1650	504	12pp	5	a Proceeding to recover $5103.3 reales, by the Royal Treasury from Da. María de León, widow of Jacinto Torres	
817	1645	504	2pp	16	Fernándo de Espinosa, rec., sues to recover $40 from José Jiménez for some samples which he brought to his store	
818	1651	506	p525	11	Fray Juan de Segueta	For having used Jewish ceremonies in order to prepare for death
819	1627	509	p80		Francisco de Acosta	(2) Pro.
820	1627	509	p193		Francisco de Acosta, a skilled mariner	Dec. answer to the accusations of Judaism made against him
821	1627	509	p318	6	Gonzálo Vaez (Port.)	(2) Pro., r. *Guadalajara* (also charged with having opened a packet of letters of S.O.)

No.	Year	Vol.	Pages	Document No.	Name of Accused or Document	Charge and Comments
822	1625	510	2pp	85	Gabriel, Jr., single (r. *Real de Cuencame*)	(2) Complaint by Bernardo de Porras
823	1690	511	113pp	1	Luis de Herrera, alias Simón Luis	(2) Test. against him
					Simón Luis, alias Luis de Herrera	(2) Test. against him
824	1690	511	pp114-280	Peru 2	Pedro Antonio Serravo	(7) Pro. relapsed
825	1661	512	84pp	2	Adan Díaz de Solis	(7) Pro., C. C.
826	1680	520	1p	34	Mateo López (Port.; dec'd)	(3) Den. by Fr. Francisco de Santa Catalina
827	1681	520	1p	41	*Fulano* Jeera	(3) Test.
828	1694	520	6pp	232	Manuel de Sosa y Prado	(1)
829	1691	526	pp242-350	a	Bernardo Duarte or Irearte	Test. for apostasy, *Acapulco*
830	1692	527	pp397-431		The 2 brothers Carrasco, alias Caravalles	(2) Inf.
831	1694	529	6pp	11	Manuel de Sosa y Prado, baker	Pro. for signs of Judaism (Port.)
832	1694	529	10pp	18	Isabel	(4) Pro., reside in *Canaria*
833	1695	530	14pp	38	Agustin Bravo *(Veracruz)*	For saying that he had stayed in the house of a Jew in Jamaica
834	1698	540	7pp	25	Miguel de Vallardes, *et al.*	(4) By Inquisitor Fiscal of the S. O.
835	1699	543	13pp	21	Pedro Legan (of *Guatemala*)	(3) By Inquisitor
836	1700	543	9pp	65	Juan de Ibernia	(3) Dec. by Miguel de Molina *(Páscuaro)*
837	1701	544	24pp	22	Pedro Henero	(2) By Fiscal of S. O.
838	1705	546	168pp	2	Andrés González de Saavedra	By Inquisitor for propositions and indications of (7)
839	1709	546	36pp	3	Andrés González de Saavedra	Inventory & sequestration of property
840	1714	551	1p	83	Four Jews	Br. Onofre Miguel del Castillo
841	1714	551	2pp	*Puebla* 84	Four Jews	Den. by Br. D. José de Mora
842	1589	558	Whole Volume		Isabel de Carvajal, widow (a/k/a Isabel Andrade, confessed 1590)	(2) Pro., C. C., daughter of Francisco Rodríguez de Matos & Da. Francisca de

No.	Year	Vol.	Pages	Document No.	Name of Accused or Document	Charge and Comments
						Carvajal, a/k/a Francisca Núñez (Port.), who were from Medina del Campo, Castile
843	1652	560	41pp	*Tulancingo* 1	Leonor de Cáceres (rec.)	(2) Pro., C. C., b. *Taxco*
844	1706	560	14pp	3	José de la Rosa (of *Tulancingo)*	Action on his petition concerning certain testimony which he gave, reneged, about being the greatgrandson of (5) and (6)
845	1695	560	6pp	7	Capt. Agustín Muñoz de Sandoval	(2) By Fiscal of the S. O., r. *Chalco*

Tomo 6 (147 pages) covers Volumes 561 to 711.

No.	Year	Vol.	Pages	Document No.	Name of Accused or Document	Charge and Comments
846	1656	569	41pp	5	Account by Juan Pimentel, merchant of Mex. City, of the sequestered property of Luis Núñez Pérez	
847	1657	572	13pp	10	Luis Pérez Roldán & another	Inventory and sequestration of property
848	1659	573	5pp	17	Diego Díaz (relaxed)	Acts about recovery of property
849	1660	578	23pp	*Oaxaca* 9	Fray Juan de Cabrera & Fray Nicolas de Cabrera	Dec. by another Fr. that these 2 had said they were descendants of suspected persons
850	1662	579	18pp	4	Francisco de Valle (Port.)	(2) Test. sent to Inq. of Seville
851	1662	582	24pp	7	Marcos del Valle	(2) Test.
852	1649	584	7pp	1	Agustin Núñez Rojas	Petition by Secretary that the Notary of Secrets send to the Accountant the papers of the accused and of the hearing before the Treasurer of doña Leonor, his wife, rec.
853	1663	584	17pp	12	Manuel Francisco	Embargo of goods made in *Xalapa, Tabasco,* belonging to penanced

No.	Year	Vol.	Pages	Document No.	Name of Accused or Document	Charge and Comments
854	1664	584	20pp	15	Juan Rodrı́guez Juárez (rec.)	Creditors proceeding against debtor
855	1667	584	12pp	17	Da. Blanca Juárez (rec.)	Royal Treasury seeks to recover the dowry which she brought to Jorge Jacinto when she married him
856	1643	585	1p	51	Juan Pérez (fled from S. O. jails)	Order for arrest & sequestration of property
857	1660	586	28pp	3	Simón Vaez Bueno, Notary of the Ecclesiastical Court of the Bishop of *Puebla*, for suspicion of being an enemy of the Holy Catholic Faith	
858	1660	587	281pp	1	Bernardo López de Mendizabal (Governor of New Mexico)	Second book of the proceso for propositions
859	1662	592	7pp	19	Cristobal Miguel (Port.)	(7) Pro. against his name and memory
860	1662	593	261pp	1	Bernardo López de Mendizabal	(4) And propositions
861	1663	594	321pp	1	Bernardo López de Mendizabal	1st hearing
862	1663	594	23pp	4	Duarte López & his brother Antonio Bravo (both Port.)	(4) R. *San Salvador, Guatemala*
863	1663	596	277pp	1	Da. Teresa de Aguilera y Roche, wife of D. Bernardo López de Mendizabal	For suspicion of the crime of Judaism
864	1663	598		19	Bernardo López de Mendizabal	Dec. of Juan Muñoz Polanco
865	1664	599	14pp	12	Pedro de Miranda (Port.) & *fulano* de Olivera	(4) b. Antequera
866	1667	606	34pp	3 a	Account of the sambenitos put in the Cathedral of Mexico City	
867	1667	606	20pp	6	Manuel de Medina (Port., tailor & r. of *Guadalajara*)	(3) C. C. & for blasphemies
868	1667	606	16pp	7	Juan Flores Ballinas, & his wife and other Port.	(4) All residents of *Chiapas*
869	1667	608	27pp	4	Fr. Cristobal de León (Manila)	For saying that he was the son of Pen. & of usurers

No.	Year	Vol.	Pages	Document No.	Name of Accused or Document	Charge and Comments
870	1768	611	20pp	4	D. Carlos Mala Espina (Genoese) & D. Juan Franco	(1) as 2d offense after heresy. Both were mine operators. *Nicaragua*
871	1669	612	274pp	1	Manuel de León (Port.)	(7) Pro., C. C.
872	1671	614	89pp	8	José de Torres and accomplices (r. *Acapulco*)	Test. by a soldier against himself & others for the crime of "Judaismo"
873	1677	633	8pp	6	Pedro de Vargas Duarte López Alvaro de Paz (all Port.)	(2) Den. by different persons residents of San Miguel, *Guatemala*
874	1682	644	273pp	3	D. Diego de Alvarado	(4) r. in *Puebla* (b. *Peru*)
875	1634	659	93pp	7	María Rodríguez (Port.) dec'd wife of Gaspar Hernández (also Port., dec'd)	(7) r. in Mexico City (rel. est. 1636; a *dogmatista*)
876	1685	660	44pp	*Sobrerete* 2	Fernando Lescano	(4) r. Royal Mines of *Chalchihuites*
877	1642	668	9pp	4	Pedro López Monforte (b. Fresnillo, rel. est. 1649)	(1) Test. of Tomás Núñez de Peralta
878	1697	668	3pp	9	A young Portuguese	(1) By Fiscal of S. O.
879	1635	670	39pp	83	Manuel Gómez de Acosta (Port., dec'd)	(2) Heretical, *New Veracruz*
880	1688	673	9pp	30	Diego de Alvardo, alias Muñoz	Against his property, rel. est. 1688
881		673	1p	51	a Model for questions to be put to witnesses for examination and proof of absence of heretics or Jews as ancestors	
882	1690	681	132pp	1	Fernanco de Medina, alias Isac de Medina (merchant)	(2) Copy of the Pro. & acts, of the Inq. of Seville
883	1691 1693	682	24pp	5,6	Captain Diego González Figueredo	(4) Merchant of *New Veracruz* & r. of *Orizaba*
884	1692	682	130pp	24	Luis de Herrera, alias Simón Luis (prisoner in secret jails of S. O.)	Inventory & sequestration of his property
885	1692	684	p476	63	Testimony taken in procesos against Jews (mention is made of Treviño and the Blancas)	
886	1692	685	p559	68	Lope de León Mendoza (Spaniard)	(3) r. in *Guadalajara*

No.	Year	Vol.	Pages	Document No.	Name of Accused or Document	Charge and Comments
887	1693	689	p174	5	D. Antonio Monteverde	(7) r. in *Zacatecas*
888	1693	689	p233		Sebastían de Salinas	(7) r. in *Zacatecas*
889	1693	689	p486	42	Manuel de León, merchant	(3) r. in *Pachuca*
890	1694	694	p140	2,3	Pedro Carretero (of noble descent), alias Pedro de la Vega, and other associates	For the crime of (2), *Puebla*
891	1694	695	p291	74	A family, Bustos, descendants of judíos	Den. by Antonio Marmolejo, r. *Villa de León*
892	1695	704	p324	3	Fernándo de Medina y Mérida, alias Morales Gómez	(2) Guilty (relaxed in person 1699) (Note: alias 882—G. O. states born "France")
893	1645	706	p420	48	Juana Enríquez, wife of Anton Vaez *(Veracruz)*	(2) Test. of Antonio Méndez Chillon

Tomo 7 (231 pages) covers Volumes 712 to 826.

No.	Year	Vol.	Pages	Document No.	Name of Accused or Document	Charge and Comments
894	1700	713	p561	59	Pedro Gutiérrez	Crime of (2); was punished by the Inq. at Lima
895	1700	713	p594	63	José González	(2)
896	1701	718	p88		Capt. D. Lope de León Mendoza y Alencastro and his brother D. José del León	(4) r. of *Durango, New Viscaya*
897	1696	718	p93	11,12	D. Lope de Mendoza y Alencastre	(3) Pro. by Inquisitor Fiscal
898	1701	718	p300		Domingo Jorge	(2) Den., r. *Veracruz*
899	1702	721	p117	7	D. Diego Núñez Viceo	(2) By Inq. Fiscal
900	1703	722	p268	10	Juan de Sola & his brother-in-law	(3) By Inq. Fiscal (b. Spain)
901	1703	722	p432	27	Lic. D. Juan Morón (a high cleric)	(1) By Inq. Fiscal, r. *Angeles (Puebla)*
902	1707	731	p260	20	Antonio de Cáceres, grandson of Luis Baez, (rel. est.)	(2) By Inq. Fiscal, b. Orense, Galicia, & r. *Puebla*
903	1711	737	p421	4	Fernando or Juan Ramírez de Guzman, calls himself Juan Antonio de León Guzman	(3) By Inq. Fiscal, r. *Guadalajara*

No.	Year	Vol.	Pages	Document No.	Name of Accused or Document	Charge and Comments
904	1712	745	p442	8	Juan Fernández de Leon, alias José Ignacio, expelled from Order of Bathlemites [a religious order established in the Americas]	(2) Account of 2d case, he was relaxed in person 1712
905	1706-1712	748	p461	5	Fr. Jose de S. Ignacio, alias Juan Fernández de León (see 904)	Account of the case— accused of heretical blasphemy & being a Jewish dogmatizer
906	1712	748	p554	13	Fr. Francisco Julio Rospillosí (of the Franciscan Order)	For having said 2 masses in one day & having business affairs with a Jew whom he should have reported
907	1714	753	p432	4	D. Alvaro Ignacio de Figueroa Ponce de León, a knight of the Military Order of Aviz	For signs or marks of being a Jew; Port.
908	1713	753	p527		Gaspar Serrano (*gachupin*, i.e., b. Spain)	(3) r. *Puebla*
909	1714	758	p428	11	(First name unknown) Barrientos, *gachupin*	He said he was penanced by the Inq. for the crime of Judaismo
910	1715	760	p509	44	D. Francisco Quiñonez	(3) r. in *Guanajuato*
911	1715	761	p569	40	Francisco de Victoria (b. Madrid)	(7) Self-denunciation and against others residing in Mexico & in Spain
912	1717	767	p276	13	D. José Pimentel (of *Acapulco*)	For signs of being a Jew
913	1717	767	p544	35	D. Lope Manuel Meléndez	Suspicion of being a descendant of a Jew, *Guanajuato*
914	1718	770	296pp	1	Basilio Perpente Joannes—Spaniard, miner at Real de *Santa Rosa de Cuisihuiriachi*	A threefold criminal— paganism, Judaism, and an apostate of various heretical sects
915	1718	772	p509	8	D. Felix Barrera, married	(3) r. Real de los *Alamos*

No.	Year	Vol.	Pages	Document No.	Name of Accused or Document	Charge and Comments
916	1718	775	p15	3	D. Manuel Ordoñez	(3) b. Seville
917	1719	777	p336	33	Juana Josefa Pimentel	Report of the case
918	1719	780	p582	12	a Report and summary of the cases against the Faith heard by S. O. with sentences for different crimes and sundry criminals since the *auto de fe* of June 16, 1715	
919	1647	785	p582	26	Acts about the relaxed, rec. and penanced from 1635	
920	1721	789	p45	3	Juan Guillermo (Irishman)	(4) r. *Puebla*
921	1721	789	p298	17	Juan Tomás la Bolta, army scout	(3) r. *Oaxaca*
922	1724	792	p301	15	D. Pedro Sánchez Manriquez Mayor of *Villa de Valles*	(3) Den., made by D. Diego Grumaldo
923*	1742*	793	p12		*Catalina Tinoco Enríquez and Diego Tinoco	(1) Test. of Pedro de Espinosa against them
924	1722	796	p207	10	Francisco García	Acts about the collection of rents & debts owed to this heretical apostate and Jew who was rec. est. by the Inq. of Seville
925	1727	817	p431	*Cuautla* 21	D. Diego de Quiñones (*gachupin;* Lieutenant)	(3) Reported by Mayor of *Villa de Jonacatepec*
926	1727	818	p84	3	D. Ventura Arnao	(3) Den. sent to the Comisario of *Ixmiquilpan*
927	1660-1728	818	p171	8	a Index of all pending causes re faith and summary of censures from 1660 to 1728	
928	1728	821	p215	14	Juan López Mejía, broker	(4) r. *Veracruz*
929	1629	823	p1	1	Francisco Pérez de Alburquerque (b. La Torre de Moncorvo, Port.)	(2) C. C., r. *Veracruz* (rec. 1630)
930	1627	823	p21	2	Francisco de Alburquerque, buyer and seller of Negroes and Alonso Holgado, pork dealer	C. C. for having gone to visit Diego Pérez de Alburquerque while a prisoner in S. O.

*Nos. 399 and 414 involve same names, in 1642.

No.	Year	Vol.	Pages	Document No.	Name of Accused or Document	Charge and Comments

Tomo 8 (200 pages) covers Volumes 827 to 870.

No.	Year	Vol.	Pages	Document No.	Name of Accused or Document	Charge and Comments
931	1731	834	p309	12	D. Antonio Calbo Diez	(3) Pharmacist
932	1731	834	p359	16	D. Juan de Vera (Spaniard), merchant	(3) Claims he was born Canary Isles
933	1732	841	p210	12	D. Gabriel Arias	(3) A *gachupin*
934	1733	848	p565		Against various Jews who practiced the Catholic Religion in *Veracruz*	Den. by Antonio Dionisio Garrote of *New Veracruz*
935	1733	848	p275		<u>a</u> *Auto de fe*, particular, held Sunday, Nov. 15, 1733, in the Church of the Convent of Santo Domingo	
936	1734	854	p180		D. Nicolas Villalta	Letter from Inq. at Seville instructing that he be sent to the Castle (prison) of San Juan de Ulua to serve the balance of 5 years of his sentence for being a Jew (Index refers to condemnation of 1738)
937	1736	859	p429		Francisco Simón, confectioner	Den. for using Jewish rites. He lived behind the Cathedral

Tomo 9 (206 pages) covers Volumes 871 to 975.

No.	Year	Vol.	Pages	Document No.	Name of Accused or Document	Charge and Comments
938	1733	873	p419	*Puebla* 14	D. José de Villauriti, alias Diego Ros. García, meat supplier for *Tlaxcala*	(4) r. in Tlaxcala
939	1739	876	p225	41	María Felipa de Alcazar (Spaniard) and many other associates of both sexes single and married	Acts of Judaism, idolatry, witchcraft, and pacts with the devil. r. *Oaxaca*
940	1746	912	p48	19	Jerónimo Pomar, born Mayorca	(1) Married in *Campeche* with María de la Vega (Spanish)
941	1759	923	p32	5	<u>a</u> About the work known as *Advice of Solomon*	

No.	Year	Vol.	Pages	Document No.	Name of Accused or Document	Charge and Comments

Tomo 10 (342 pages) covers Volumes 975 to 1111.

No.	Year	Vol.	Pages	Document No.	Name of Accused or Document	Charge and Comments
942	1758	976	p216	61	a Order of the S. O. sending the 4-vol. *History of the Jews* by Samuel Basnague, in French, for expurgation to *calificador,* who examines books	
943	1755	978	p337	23	D. Miguel de Espejo	(3) r. in *Jalapa*
944	1758	979	p238	12	a Denunciation of Basnague's *History of Jews* (see 942)	
945	1759	991		2	Juan Tibel & Isac Salomon	S. O. acknowledges receipt of reconciliations
946	1765-1782	1002	p283	21	D. Juan Laureano de Burgos, Mayor of *Zacualpa*	(2) And indications of heresy. Decs. & Test. Autograph of D. José de la Bordo
947	1769	1017	p172	4	a Den. of 3 small volumes, *Secret Memoirs of the Republic of Letters* (in French) by the author of Jewish letters	
948	1785	1032	p127	7	José Uruzel of Brusal, First Musician of the Regiment of the Crown	(3) By Inq. Fiscal of S. O. (French)
949	1761	1033	p384	19	José Gil Taboada, Mayor of *S. Juan Teotihuacán*	(3) Investigation
950	1765	1038	p297	5	Juan Angelini, soldier in the Regiment of The America	(2) And heresy. Test. of the Inq. of Zaragoza & Barcelona
951	1764	1041	p92	11	Nicolás Martinez (b. in Greece)	(3) Candlemaker with store on S. Francisco St.
952	1768	1052	p415	29	José Salomón, doctor	(3) *Guatemala*
953	1779	1108	p137	Oaxaca	Esteban Zerecedo (Spanish), married to Tomasa Olivares	(4) And superstitious acts, r. *Tlacolula*

Tomo 11 (254 pages) covers Volumes 1083 to 1169.

(Volumes 1083 to 1111 inclusive are carbon copies of what appears in Tomo 10 and constitutes pages 1 to 93 of Tomo 11)

No.	Year	Vol.	Pages	Document No.	Name of Accused or Document	Charge and Comments
954	1778	1133	p420	18	D. Agustín de Espinola, merchant	(4) He was seen in attendance at the Synagogue in Kingston, Jamaica

No.	Year	Vol.	Pages	Document No.	Name of Accused or Document	Charge and Comments
955	1772	1145	p28	3	D. Santiago Azcazibar, also known as D. Santiago Raymundi y Arengo, surgeon	He said he was a Jew. He pretended to marry a second time while first wife alive; r. S. *José del Parral, Chihuahua*
			p43		Inventory of his property	
956	1729	1169	p98	8	D. Gerardo Moro, attorney for the Royal Court	(1) Den. by D. María de Contreras Villegas; also charged as enemy of religious practices

Tomo 12 (208 pages) covers Volumes 1170 to 1250.

No.	Year	Vol.	Pages	Document No.	Name of Accused or Document	Charge and Comments
957	1775	1171	p126	6	José María Caldes	For feigning to be a Jew and a Protestant, r. *Guadalajara*
958	1735	1175	p1	1	D. José de Cárdenas, Mayor of *Tecali* (near Puebla)	For saying that he was circumcised
959	1735	1175	p298	30	D. José de Cárdenas	(1) By Inq. Fiscal of S. O.
960	1780	1203	p347	22	José Antonio Fernández, a soldier in the 2d Inf. Regiment	For not being baptized & being circumcized
961	1788	1234	p67		D. Rafael Gil Rodríguez, Franciscan monk or minor priest (circumcised)	(2) And formal heresy—Sta. Ana Grande, *Guatemala* (rec. 1795)

Tomo 13 (212 pages) covers Volumes 1253 to 1336.

No.	Year	Vol.	Pages	Document No.	Name of Accused or Document	Charge and Comments
962	1783	1283	p75	5	D. Manuel Vázquez, mayor of *Pánuco* and *Tampico* (for further reference see 963, which follows)	(4) And for reading possessing books of Voltaire and other prohibited authors, and for propositions and superstitions. (Many interesting features)
963					(No. 962 was a continuation of an earlier case which is found at pp67, 68 of vol. 1283, #3, but is not separately indexed)	
964	1796	1313		7	a Minutes of S.O. listing punishments and garroting	

No.	Year	Vol.	Pages	Document No.	Name of Accused or Document	Charge and Comments

Tomo 14 (195 pages) covers Volumes 1337 to 1409.

965					a Volume 1396 has several Royal decrees during the year 1813 about the abolition of the Tribunal of the Inquisition. In 1814 and July 31, 1815, the reestablishment of the Tribunal of the Santo Oficio was decreed	
966	1820	1397	p221	16	a List of the various cases from 1800 to 1820	
967	1802	1408	p1	1	Edict from the Inquisitor General made in Comayagua (made from the new orders) to the Comisarios of all parts and in the Capital prohibiting the entry of Jews—*Edict. of Sept. 16, 1802*, found at pp 2 and 3	
968	1802	1408	p106	13	a 2 volumes of Flavius Josephus, *Bello Judaico* are detained at the Royal Custom House, addressed to a monk. His Vicar applies for entry of the books	
969	1771-1803	1408	p265	23	a Index of all cases and papers from 1771 to 1803 with a report of status on cases which were on the table of Secretary Najera	

Tomo 15 (256 pages) covers Volumes 1410 to 1460.

[Actually, this Tomo covers to Volume 1552, the volumes 1470 to 1544 being part of the Collection of Riva Palacio. These are separately indexed in the *Boletin del Archivo General de la Nación*, Tomo IV, Sept. Oct. 1933, No. 5; and Nov. Dec. 1933, No. 6. The cases of Jewish interest are appended to this compilation and the volume numbers used are those of the Riva Palacio Collection and are the ones that appear in the two issues of the Bulletin mentioned above.]

970	1795	1416	p144		a an unnamed husband	Den. by his wife because he was affected by French liberty and for saying that the best law was that of the Jews
971	1804	1422	p128	15	a Index of all cases 1780-1803 which were on the table of Secretary Lic. Torrecilla, with status of each	
972	1805	1429	p59		a Request made for the entry of 2 cases of books of which 2 volumes were "Customs of the Israelites and Christians." Request by D. Mateo Mosso, merchant. Sent from *Veracruz*	
973	1626	1552	p100		Antonio Fernández (Port.)	(3) r. *San Luis Potosí*
974	1626	1552	p155		Luisa González, mulato	Jewish rites
975	1626	1552	p299		Maestro Pedro de Arizmendi, Palomeno Gogorrón	Descendants of Jews

Index to the *Riva Palacio Collection*

Taken from Tomo IV, No. 5 (September-October, 1933), of the
Boletin del Archivo General de la Nación.

No.	Year	Vol.	Document No.	Name of Accused or Document	Charge and Comments
976		3	2	a Instructions to Comisarios on matters of faith	
977	1601-1616	7	2	a Letters from S. O. of Spain to New Spain with alphabetical index	
978		9		a Practical material on crimes and cases against faith made by Dr. Isidoro de San Vicente of the Supreme Council	
979	1571	10	1	a Acts read and done re S. O. in Cathedral	
980	1589	11	2	Luis de Carvajal, the younger, bachelor, merchant (confessed 1590)	(2) 1st case, b. Villa de Benavente, Castile—son of Francisco Rodríguez Matos & Francisca Carvajal
981	1589	11	3	Luis Carvajal, Governor of New Kingdom of León	Pro., b. Villa de Mogodorio, Port.
982	1589	12	1	D. Francisca de Caravajal, widow of Francisco Rodríguez de Matos. She is of the generation of new Christians of Jews	(2) Pro., b. Villa de Mogodorio, Port., near Benavente, Castile
983	1589	12	2	Leonor de Andrada, wife of Jorge de Almayda	Pro., b. Villa de Benavente, of generation of new Christians of Jews (relaxed in person—per Medina, p. 174)
984	1589	12	3	Baltazar Rodríguez de Andrada or De Carbajal, younger, bachelor, son of Francisco Rodríguez de Matos and Da Francisca de Carvajal, Port.	(2) Pro., b. Benavente, Castile
985	1589	12	4	Diego Marcos de Andrada	(2) Pro.
986	1595	13	1	Isabel Rodríguez, wife of Manuel Díaz	(2) Pro., b. Salceda, Port.
987	1595	13	2	Manuel Díaz, merchant	(2) Pro., b. Fondón, Port.
988	1595	13	3	Sebastian Rodríguez	(2) Pro., b. San Vicente, Port.

No.	Year	Vol.	Document No.	Name of Accused or Document	Charge and Comments
989	1595	14		Luis de Carvajal	(2) Pro., 2d, having been rec. in 1st Pro.
990	1595	15	1	Antonio López (fugitive; rel. est. 1596)	(2) Pro., b. Celorico, Port.
991	1595	15	2	Antonio López, son of Diego López Ragalón	(2) Pro., b. Seville, musician and singer in comedies (rec. 1601)
992	1596	15	3	Mariana de Carvajal, maiden daughter of Francisco Rodríguez de Matos & Da. Francisca de Carvajal	(2) Pro. her father rel. est. for observing the dead Law of Moses, b. Benavente
993	1596	16	1	Marco Antonio, young bachelor	(2) Pro., b. Cubillana, Port.
994	1596	16	2	Domingo Cuello	(2) Pro., b. Braga, Port.
995	1596	16	3	Antonio Machado, dec'd	(2) Pro., against his name & memory, b. Lisbon, Port.
996	1597	17	2	Francisco Rodríguez de Ledezma	(2) Pro., b. Barcuelo, Pardo, 10 leagues from Ledezma
997	1598	17	3	Antonio Méndez (Port.)	(2) Pro., reared in Jeva, Andalucia, near *Pachuca*
998	1598	18	1	Jorge Alvarez	Pro. for concealing real identity of himself & others, b. Fondón, Port.
999	1599	18	2	a Gaspar de Los Reyes Plata Constable of the S. O. secret jails	For excesses (he is not Jewish)
1000	1602	18	3	Clara Enríquez, maiden	(2) Pro., daughter of Manuel de Lucena, relaxed in person
1001	1604	18	4	Manuel Rodríguez (Port.)	Reconciled for (7); for riding a horse with saddle & bridle and using prohibited things
1002	1591	18	5	Lic. Miguel Franco, doctor	(4) Pro., b. Aveto, Port.
1003	1604	20	2	Justa Méndez (Port.)	(7) Pro., previously rec.
1004	1625	20	5	Tomás Treviño	(2) C. C., b. Medina de Rio Seco
1005	1647	20	6	Leonor Martínez, daughter of Tomás Treviño & María Gómez, both rec.	Pro., C. C.

No.	Year	Vol.	Document No.	Name of Accused or Document	Charge and Comments
1006	1646	23	2	María de Campos	(2) Pro., C. C., b. Montemer, Port.
1007		25		Da. María de Zarate, wife of Francisco Botello (relaxed in person)	(2) C. C. (r. *Tacubaya*; rec. 1659)
1008	1601	35	5,6,7,16	a Report of auto general celebrated Mar. 25, 1601	
1009	1667	35	17	a Report of the sambenitos hung in Cathedral in 1667	
1010		43	3	a Formula or pattern for procesos and criminal cases against prisoners of the Inq.	
1011	1719	49		a General Index of all cases of faith which had been prosecuted by S. O. of Mexico from 1571 to 1719	

[Continuation of the Index to the Collection of Riva Palacio according to Tomo IV, No. 6 (November-December, 1933) of the *Boletin del Archivo General de la Nación*. This is the conclusion to the first part which appears. This issue is in the form of an alphabetical Index. Only cases involving Jews or of Jewish interest appear below]

No.	Year	Vol.	Case No.	Information
1012	1589	11	2	Luis de Carvajal, el mozo, first proceso. (Repetition of No. 980)
1013	1595	14		Luis de Carvajal, el mozo, second case. (Repetition of No. 989)

(Both of these cases plus young Carvajal's memoirs and letters constitute Vol. XXVIII of the *Publicaciones del Archivo General de la Nación* (México, 1935.)

1014		49		Cases of faith in the General Index of the Inquisition in Mexico. (Repetition of 1011)
1015		52		Jurisdiction of the Inquisition of Mexico

At page 917 of the aforesaid *Boletin*, appears the heading "Appendix to the Index to the Riva Palacio Collection"

1016	1590	55	11	(3) Pro., against Julian de Castellanos, foreman born Xarandilla. (Confessed 1590)
1017	1596	55	3	(2) Pro., against Isabel Machado, maiden daughter of Antonio Machado dec'd (rec. 1601)
1018	1696	55	4	(Date should be 1956.) (Nature of crime not stated.) Pro. against Alvaro de Carrión, b. Cervera de Rio Pisuegra, Port. r. at *Tilcuatla*, near *Pachuca*, married. (Heretical Jew; rec. 1601)
1019	1642	56	3	(7) Pro., C. C. against D. Blanca Méndez de Rivera, widow of Diego López Rivero, b. Seville
1020	1642	57	1	(7) Pro., against Violante Texosso, maiden, b. *Lima, Peru*, r. *Veracruz*, 19 years of age
1021	1642	68		Test. of Blanca de Rivera against many other Jews
1022				Page 929 of *Boletin* - Alphabetical name index

Appendix A

Alfonso Toro

Los Judíos en la Nueva España is the title of Volume **XX** of the Publications of the AGN. It was prepared by Alfonso Toro, a Mexican historian and paleographer. Part 2 of the book contains a list of Jews before the Inquisition in the sixteenth century. This Appendix covers only those who do not appear in the preceding pages. A comparison has been made of the cases set forth by Toro with his citations in the Volume of Documents and the case number in the Indice. He never cited the *Indice*.

Toro wrote that the ideas of many people accused of blasphemy were "de judíos o judaizantes" (of Jews or those who practiced Judaism, p. 86). In other words, there were many more Jews in Mexico than those who were apprehended by the Inquisition and many of those whose crime was "blasphemy" were Jews.

He lists cases "for causes of faith," which included blasphemy, on pages 91 to 161. None of these are contained herein unless there was clear proof of the charge or existence of Judaism.

The book contains many cases of non-Jews, which makes the title of the book slightly deceptive. The book has no name index.

No.	Year	Toro	Indice del Ramo de Inquisicion
1023	1554	(Jan.) Vol. 30, case #11, Juan de Astarga, sospechoso de judío.	To. 1, p28; 8pp., same accused and date. A proceso of the Ecclesiastical Court. Born in Seville. A clogmaker, "for having found in his house a cross in a clog between the cork and the sole."
1024	1554	(Oct.) Vol. 30, case #13, Diego de Briones por sospechoso de judío. (The Indice does not list this case in this volume.)	1554. Inf. brought against Hernándo de Cazalla. (See #17 main index.)
1025	1556	(Oct.) Vol. 30, #1, Blas Mosquera, judío, hitting a priest.	1564 (To. 1, p.28.) Pro. against Nicolas Mosquera, bomber of the ship, "The Good Angel," for striking a priest. (There is a difference in the first names.)
1026	1521	(Oct.) Vol. 49, #1, Antonio Sañer, heretical Jew	(To. 1, p43.) Pro. against Martín Arana. (See #22 main index.)
1027	No date;	Vol. 50, Pierres Aufroy, French, heresy and Jew. (Note that Toro lists this case on p9 of his book but later at pp55 and 71, where the same accused appears, Toro asserts only "lutheranism.")	1571 (p44 of To. 1 of the *Indice.*) Same accused but name spelled Pierres Ampoy, pirate, for Lutheranism.
1028	1572	(Jan.) Vol. 51, #1, Pedro Chartre, French, for heresy and suspicion of Jew.	(P44 of To. 1.) Accused Pedro Ocharte, suspected of Lutheranism, 70pp.

No.	Year	Tomo	*Indice del Ramo de Inquisicion*
1029	1572	(Mar.) Vol. 52, #1, Gaspar de los Reyes, for Jew.*	(P44 of To. 1.) Same date and accused, a pharmacist but "for blasphemy."
1030	1580	(Feb.) Vol. 125, #4, Alejandra Testa (for heresy and being a Jewess).	(P111 of To. 1.) 1539, Den. against Pedro Núñez, candlemaker, for perjury. 1p. (Note—a search of the Indice pp111 to 116 incl. fails to reveal any accused named Testa.)
1031	1581	(Jan.) Vol. 126, #1, Andrés Ruiz Esparaza for heresy and suspicion of Jew.	(P116 of To. 1.) Same date and accused but crime "for suspicion of Lutheranism."
1032	1592	(June) Vol. 150, #5, Domingo Jorge, suspected of being a Jew.	(P142 of To. 1.) Same date, Inf. against Domingo and Juan Rodríguez, brothers, for their manner of living and suspicious words, 33pp, Manila.
1033	1594	(July) Vol. 151, #2, Daniel Sastre suspicion of heresy and Jew. [Note: sastre means a tailor. Toro refers at p65 of his book to Daniel Benitez and attributes his birthplace to Hamburg.]	(P143 of To. 1.) Same date, Pro. against Castro, other name Juan, born in Hamburg, for suspicion of Lutheranism, 7pp, reside in Tecamachalco. However, case #3, immediately following the above, is against Daniel Benitez, a tailor (see #60 of main index) born in Borgñon, residing in *Tecamachalco*.
1034	1597	(Mar.) Vol. 161, #3, Pro. against Juan Lozano, Jew.	(P146, To. 1.) Same date and accused but crime is "blasphemy." Resides in *Puebla*.
1035	1597	(Mar.) Vol. 161, #4, Pro. against Luis Sandoval, Jew.	(P146, To. 1.) Same date and accused but crime "blasphemy," 9pp.
1036	1597	(May) Vol. 161, #5, Pro. against Juan, negro; Jew. [Note: Toro also lists this case under Vol. 161, case #7. In the Indice this would correspond to the charge of denying God, Tlaxcala #10.]	(P146, To. 1.) Same date. Accused is Juan Criollo, negro born in Mexico, slave of Cristobal de Cuenca, officer of the mint, "for having blasphemed," 21pp.
1037	1597	(May) Vol. 161, #7, Pro. against Francisco Maderos, Jew.	(P146, To. 1.) Same date, accused last name, "Medero," innkeeper in the town of *"Sichu of the Indians,"* born in la Breña, close to Paloma in the Canaries. (There is no statement of any crime.)

1038   The name Juan Bautista Corvera (also Cervera) does not appear in the *Indice* or in any case of Jewish interest. Toro refers to him on page xxviii of "Los Judíos," etc., and states that a proceso "por judaizante" was instituted against him. From page 181 to 187 of the book, Toro sets forth various poems and sonnets that were among the compositions taken from Bautista and which led to his difficulty with the Inquisition. Toro has failed to give the location of the proceso or the poetry in any of the Document Volumes. It should be noted that neither J. T. Medina nor Julio Jiménez Rueda list him in their alphabetical index of the *Historía del Tribunal de la Inquisición*.

---

*José Toribio Medina, *Historía del Tribunal,* etc., p. 61, states that Gaspar de los Reyes, b. Seville, was in the auto of Feb. 1574 and was the grandson of "relaxed."

In *Los Judíos en la Nueva España,* Toro lists the names of those condemned between 1528 and 1637. This information came from Document Volume 77, p64, as noted in Item 33 of the foregoing *Guide.* Toro lists many names other than those of Jews. The following names are only those not otherwise found in this *Guide.* [Rios is an abbreviation for Rodríguez. Toro never indicates this and uses both names.] The first number is that in this *Guide* while the second and smaller number is that used by Toro.

1039 #1.   Hernándo Alonso Herrero [herrero is also an occupation and from other sources, it is believed that Toro erred], born Condado de Niebla, heretical Judaizante, relaxed in person 1528.

1040 #2.   Gonzálo de Morales, shopkeeper, born Seville of Jewish parents, heretical Judaizante, relaxed in person 1528.

1041 #3.   Diego de Ocaña, scribe, born Seville of Jewish parents, heretical judaizante, reconciled 1528.

1042 (p52)   Gabriel Rios, born Cercedas, Port., merchant in *Zacatecas,* of Jewish
#43.   parents, heretical judaizante, reconciled 1591.

1043 #44.   Francisco Ruiz de Luna, born Cordoba, heretical judaizante. Reconciled 1591.

1044 #57.   Miguel Rodríguez, brother of Luis, el mozo, son of Francisco Rodríguez Matos and Doña Francisca Núñez, heretical judaizante, relaxed in estatua 1596.

1045 #62.   Andrés Rios, born Fondon, Port., merchant reside in *Tezcuco,* heretical Judaizante, reconciled 1576.

1046 #64.   Isabel Pérez, wife of Manuel de Morales, heretical judaizante. Rel. est. 1596.

1047 #65.   Antonio Rodríguez, Port., deceased, bachelor, born San Vicente Davera, heretical judaizante. Rel. est. 1596.

1048 #68.   Diego Enríquez, reconciled for heretical judaizante, son of Beatriz Enríquez la Paiba and Simon Paiba. Relaxed in person 1596.

1049 #72.   Domingo Rios, reconciled for heretical judaizante; relapsed for same crime. Rel. est. in 1596.

1050 #74.   Fabian Granados, born Lamego, Port., heretical judaizante. Rel. est. 1596.

1051 #83.   Manuel Francisco de Belmonte, born Cuvillana, Port., reside *Sultepeque;* heretical judaizante. Reconciled 1596.

1052 #84.   Violante Ríos, widow of Simón González, born Salceda, Port., heretical judaizante. Reconciled 1596.

1053 #88.   Pedro Ríos, born Fondon, Port., heretical judaizante. Reconciled 1596 (See No. 132).

1054 #113.   Da. Ana de Carbajal, maiden daughter of Francisco Rodríguez de Matos and Francisca de Carabajal, heretical judaizante. Reconciled 1601.

1055 #119.   Inés Fernández, wife of Francisco Alvarez and sister of Manuel Morales; heretical judaizante. Rel. est. 1601.

1056 #120.   Jorge Díaz, silversmith, Port., heretical judaizante. Rel. est. 1601.

1057 #125.   Leonor de Cázares, daughter of Antonio Díaz de Cázares, Port., and Catalina de León, a relaxed Jewess. Reconciled 1601.

1058 #126.   Lorenzo Machado, Port., born Villa Villanueva de Portiman, resident of the mines of *San Luis.* Reconciled 1601.

1059 #127.   Luis Díaz, silversmith, heretical judaizante. Rel. est. 1601.

1060 #131.   Manuel Gómez Silvera, Port., born Moron, reside mines of *Sultepec*.
              Reconciled 1601.

1061 #134.   Pelayo Alvarez, Port., born Freixo de Espadacinta, heretical judaizante.
              Reconciled in estatua 1601.

1062 #155.   Marco Antonio (see 188 of Index), born Castelo-Blanco, Port., heretical
              judaizante. Reconciled 1596.

1063 #47.   (p73) Hernán Rodríguez de Herrera, born Fondon, Port., heretical
              judaizante. Reconciled 1590.

1064 #178.   (p82) Domingo de Sousa, born Lisbon, Port., heretical judaizante.
              Reconciled in estatua 1626.

Appendix B

Luis González Obregón and José Toribio Medina

There are many other sources of information about Mexican Colonial Jews outside the AGN. Many documents are in private possession and others are scattered over the world in university libraries, museums and institutions, some uncatalogued. Luis González Obregón, in *México Viejo*, has an Appendix of forty pages which is a copy of a list made by P. Pichardo of the *sambenitos* and *tabillas* hanging in the Mexican Cathedral. Many new names and pertinent data appear that have been added to the present compilation. The additions are not in the AGN. An attempt has been made to avoid repetitions. The Appendix in *México Viejo* contains several errors (which have been deleted where noted) and much misspelling. This has hindered the "weeding-out" process.

In *Historía del Tribunal del Santo Oficio del la Inquisición en México*, with additions by Julio Jiménez Rueda, there is an alphabetical list of those who appeared before the Santo Oficio. Jiménez Rueda made his additions from AGN records. We do not know the source of all of Medina's information. Some of it was garnered in Spain. The same process had been utilized for this list as with González Obregón. Genaro García has no names which do not appear in either of the two books cited.

Unless otherwise indicated, both books are in accord and the charge is "heretical judaizante." If disagreement exists: M = Medina and G. O. = González Obregón; and if the name appears in only one of the books, then the initial will be used.

1065 *Garcia Gonzalez Bermeguero.* Born in Albuquerque. His two brothers, their wives, and his uncle had been relaxed in Llerena, Spain, for being Jews. The Inquisition there wrote to Mexico. He was 70 years of age when arrested July 6, 1579, was poor and the father of several children, among whom was an Augustinian monk. He was relaxed in person October 11, 1579, and his property confiscated.

1066 *Catalina de León.* Reconciled 1590, wife of Gonzálo Pérez Ferro and first cousin once removed of *Francisca Núñez de Carvajal* who had a daughter of the same name (see 1067).

1067 *Catalina de León de la Cueba*, wife of *Antonio Días Casare*, daughter of Francisca Núñez de Carvajal, burned at stake 1596.

1068 (G. O.) *Francisca Ullis de Luna.* Born Cordoba; confessed 1591.

1069 (M.) *Francisco Ruiz de Luna,* also known as Fray Francisco de Luna. Observer of the Law of Moses, reconciled; 200 lashes, ten years in galley, perpetual jail and sambenito. He had been placed in the cell with *Luis de Carvajal,* el mozo, in order to convert him but was himself converted to Judaism by the young Carvajal.

1070 (M.) *Melchor Juárez* (secretary to Bishop Palafox). He was denounced by a woman in whose house he lived. She and her whole family were observers of the Law of Moses and were in the S. O. prisons. They also said that Juárez was the brother of a Jew relaxed in the auto of 1601 in Llerena. Testimony came from Llerena that Juárez's wife had died in jail there while awaiting trial for being a Jewess. The Judges in Mexico found nothing substantial touching on Melchor Juárez (see letter of Sept. 20, 1644, AGN).

1071 *Jorge* and *Domingo Rodríguez* (M.); *Jorge* and *Domingo Rios* (G. O.). Jorge born in Seville and Domingo in Fondon (Port.); both young bachelors, residents of

Manila. They were of "new Christians." They were brought from Manila to Mexico and were in the auto of 1593. (M.)—"They observed all the rites, precepts, and ceremonies of Jews and awaited the Messiah. They confessed under threat of torture, reconciled with loss of all their goods and to perpetual jail." Jorge was arrested again in 1601 and again reconciled, not relaxed, because he made a speedy confession. (Note: There is no explanation of how he acquired more goods and was out of jail.)

1072 Lic. *Manuel de Morales*. A *"dogmatista"* (see Glossary). He had been a principal ringleader of the Jews who had been penitenced in the auto of Feb. 24, 1590. He escaped and was burned in effigy in 1593. (See Carta de García March 17, 1594; AGN.)

1073 *Francisco Rios Matos*. "Dogmatista"; confessed and relaxed in 1591. He had been in the auto of Feb. 24, 1590, reconciled then with confiscation of property because he "kept and believed the dead law of Moses and observed their ritual, celebration of Passover, fasted, observed Sabbaths, and hoped for the coming of the Messiah which would give them (Jews) wealth and raise them to glory, believing that Jesus was not the Messiah, his law a lie, a thing of air."

1074 *Manuel Díaz*. Brother of *Andrez Rodríguez*, previously reconciled. Relaxed in person in 1596 for being an obdurate denier. He was son-in-law of *Violante Rodríguez*.

1075 *Beatriz Enríquez*, wife of Simón Payba, mother of *Catalina, Diego Enríquez* (burned 1596 after relapse) *Pedro Enríquez* (reconciled 1596), was considered the *"greatest dogmatizadora"* among all the women exclusive of the Carvajal family. She was burned in the auto de fe 1596. She was the mother-in-law of *Manuel de Lucena*. He and three of her children testified against her.

1076 (M. only) *Clara de Rivera*. Died in jail and reconciled en estatua in the auto of April 16, 1646 "for being a Jew."

1077 *Margarita de Morera*. Reconciled for being a Jew (1646) and condemned to sambenito. She testified that a negro dressed in a red suit went through the streets playing a tambourine which was the signal for all Jews to assemble. She was the daughter of *Pascual de Morera*, postmaster (Port.), and *Catalina Díaz de Rosas*, Jews.

1078 *Diego López*. Born San Vicente Davera, Port.; young bachelor, heretical judaizante. Reconciled 1596. M. states that later he received 100 lashes for entering the "houses of the Santo Oficio."

1079 *Isabel Rodríguez*. Wife of *Manuel Días* (relaxed) born Salceda, Port. and daughter of *Violante Rios*. Reconciled 1596.

1080 (M. only) *Clara Enríquez*. Daughter of *Manuel de Lucena*. Observing law of Moses. She confessed after threat of torture and was in the auto of April 1603.

1081 *Clara Enríquez*. Widow of Francisco Méndez, born Fondon, Port. Reconciled 1596.

1082 (G. O. only) *Pedro Riosas*. Born Fondon; reconciled 1596.

1083 *Juan Rodriguez de Silva*. Port.; young bachelor, fugitive. Burned in effigy 1596.

1084 (M. only) *Diego Díaz Nieto*. Born Ferrera, Italy. He was denounced as a Jew in 1596, released and rearrested in 1601. He came to New Spain with his father under Bull of Clement VIII and a license of the King (of Spain) to seek charity. The most learned people of Mexico were sent by the S. O. to confront him. They were bested by him and they admired the nimbleness of his answers and his intellect. He finally asked to be baptized and confessed that his previous reconciliation was feigned. He requested alms to return to Italy. However, testimony against him began to grow and he was sentenced in the auto of April 1603 to perpetual jail, unpardonable; never to speak to anyone under penance of the S. O. and for two years to be a recluse in a monastery. (Note: The S. O. used "convento" to signify monastery as well as convent.)

1085 *Tomás Fonseca.* He was 80 years old when he appeared in the auto of 1601 and very sick. G. O. states he was relaxed in person. M. states perpetual jail and loss of property.

1086 *Tomás Fonseca de Castellano.* He was 52 years of age in the auto of 1601; a relapso; and in the torture chamber confessed that he had observed the Law of Moses with a friend (unnamed). He was burned alive and although he 'made demonstration of dying as a Christian, it was with great coolness."

1087 *Bernardo de Luna.* Resident of *Michoacan;* reconciled 1601 with perpetual jail, 200 lashes and confiscation of goods. He was not sent to the galleys because he was 'very bad."

1088 (G. O. only) *Francisco Rodríguez Desa.* Born San Vicente Davera, husband of *Leonor Días,* burned in effigy 1601.

1089 (M. only) *Juan Machada.* Doctor, son of *Antonio Machado.* (His name does not appear in M's Index.) He was summoned for the remains of his father's corpse burned in the auto of 1601.

1090 (M. only) *Francisco Rodríguez.* See 1091.

1091 *Francisco Rodríguez.* There were two individuals with identical names burned in effigy in the auto of March 25, 1601. They were both Portuguese and disciples of the Law of Moses. (M. gives no further information.)

1092 *Francisco Rodríguez de Ledesma.* Born town of Salamanco (this differs from No. 996) of caste of new Christians. At page 171, M. states that he was from Toledo. He was in the auto of March 1601 and confessed to being a Jew before the reading of the sentence. He was remanded to jail and appears again in the auto of April 20, 1603. He confessed after being advised that he was to be tortured. While in jail, he became gravely ill and died. He was burned in effigy.

1093 *Juan Rodríguez.* Port.; tavern-keeper; fugitive and relaxed in estatua 1601.

1094 (a) *Melchor Rodríguez de Encina.* (M. only.) Resided in *Puebla.* For saying that the Comisario of the S. O. in Puebla was a "young Jewish dog" and that he ought to receive 1000 blows. He was tried but never appeared in any auto, nor does M. give his sentence. He was tried c. 1601.

1095 *Simón Payba,* also known as *Simón Rodríguez Payba.* Born in Lisbon and processed for heretical judaizante and his bones disinterred from grave and burned in the auto of 1601. (Note: All entries in the AGN Indice contain references to his family but there are no entries concerning his proceso.)

1096 (G. O.) *Juan Antonio Doria.* Born in Mexico and was in charge of coining for the Royal Mint. Reconciled 1601.

1097 *Mariana Núñez,* also known as *Mariana de Carvajal* (G. O. spells her name Munos). She was 16 years old in the auto of 1590. She and other members of her family escaped being 'relaxed" because they confessed, gave demonstrations of grief and repentance (or conversion). She was 29 years old in 1601 (per M.), unmarried, and was burned at the stake after repentance and conversion. She had tranquilly confessed to all the charges and many others. "The people were satisfied with her conversion and good death."

1098 *Juana Magdalena,* mulatto born near *Topatolcingo,* wife of *Joseph de Valencia,* a Jewish resident of *Tetclan.* Reconciled 1603.

1099 (G. O.) *Domingo Díaz,* also known as *Domingo Rodríguez,* son of *Sebastian* and *Costanza Rios.,* heretical judaizante. Reconciled 1625.

1100 (M.) *Domingo Rodríguez*. Previously reconciled and was dead for four years when his body was disinterred, burned in effigy Dec. 8, 1596, and his property confiscated. He was denounced for not confessing to [observance] of the fast of Queen Esther. He had a brother Antonio, condemned for same reasons, same fate, same time.

1101 (**G. O.**) *Domingo Fernández*. Born La Torre Moncorbo, Port; confessed 1635.

1102 *Leonor Núñez*. Born Madrid and was in the auto of April 1635; a daughter of new Christians; wife of Diego Fernández Cardado and later of Pedro López alias *Simón Fernández*, both husbands deceased and both were Hebrew Christians. She had been denounced in *Peru* for observing Law of Moses. In 1635, she was reconciled, sentenced to sambenito and jail for 2 years and loss of her property. She was burned in person in the Grand Auto of April 11, 1649, together with her daughters *Ana* and *María Gómez*, her son *Francisco López Blandon*, and her sister *Isabel Núñez*, 42 years of age. Ana was 43, Francisco 31 and María 32 when they went to the stake. (M. has nothing to indicate husbands of Leonor. Her marital history comes from G. O.)

1103 *Antonio Vaez Tirado*. Port., relaxed in person in the auto of 1648 (G. O. 1649) when he was 75 years of age. He had been reconciled in the auto of 1625. He *"passed as a rabbi among the Jews of Mexico."* (M. pp119, 204). He was a brother of *Simon Vaez Sevilla*.

1104 *Pedro López* alias *Simón Fernández*. Resided Mexico City and *Ixmiquilpan* (see 1102). His body was disinterred for burning in the auto of April 1635 because he was convicted of heretical judaizante, a *"dogmatista"* and a teacher of the Law of Moses.

1105 *Manuel Xuárez* (M. spells "Juarez"), deceased; Port. of Mexico City and *Veracruz*, husband of *Ana Fernández* also deceased, Jews. Both burned in effigy 1635.

1106 *Baltazar Díaz del Valle*. Merchant of *Pachuca*, was reconciled at the auto of April 1635 with confiscation of his property, condemned to sambenito and perpetual jail plus 100 lashes. His wife *Isabel López Cardado* was put twice into the rack, confessed to Jewish practices. She received the same sentence as her husband, except no lashes, and died in jail within two months.

1107 *Antonio López Blandón*. Born Madrid, resided in *Guadalajara;* heretical Jew; burned in effigy 1635; also termed a *dogmatist* and teacher of the law of Moses.

1108 Antonio López de Orduña. 20 years of age (Genaro García says 26 and that he confessed being a Jew). Born Seville; circumcised; merchant in *Guadalajara,* deceased at time of auto; assistant to the mayor of *Chichicapa;* bachelor; son of a Portuguese father and mother from Seville (both new Christians). (Note: Interesting burial customs for Jews. J. Jiménez Rueda states that a certain passage was worthy of comparison with an etching by don Francisco de Goya de Lucientes.) He was reconciled with sambenito in the auto of April 16, 1646. (García says he was son of *Fernando Vaez de Torres* who was born in Casteloblanco and died in Utrera, but mother, Isabel Rodríguez, was born in Seville.)

1109 *Simón Juárez de Espinosa*. Born and lived in Mexico City. He was converted to Judaism in order to marry doña *Juana de Tinoco* "and in order to make more expedient or to facilitate his apostasy, they took him to the Cathedral and showed him the sambenito of her grandfather." He was a traveling merchant. His wife *Juana* was the reconciled daughter of *Julio Xuárez de Figueroa* (Port.) and of *Anna Espinosa* of Mexico City, daughter of *Simón Rios*. Ana was reconciled "Jew." He confessed 1646.

1110 *Juana del Bosque*. Mulatto; born in Cartagena (S. A.); wife of *Blas López* (Port.), a fugitive; daughter of *Esperanza Rodríguez* (reconciled) and of *Juan Baptista*, a German; confessed and reconciled in 1646 together with her sister *Isabel del Bosque*. Juana was 29 years old at the time. Both sisters were seamstresses.

1111 *Jerónimo Núñez* alias de Rojas. He was a half brother of *Agustín de Rojas*. He was a descendant of "new Hebrew Christians." He was reconciled in 1646. M. comments that Gabriel de Granada was circumcised "when small (young) by a certain famous rabino who moved through the King's realm, Jerónimo Núñez." He tried to present a claim against the property of Agustín [while Agustín was in Inquisition jail and his property confiscated by the S. O.] with a false date on the evidence of indebtedness, predating it prior to Agustín's incarceration [so that he could collect as a creditor]. *Agustin de Rojas* was the husband of *Leonor Vaez* (Port.) and hanged himself in the S. O. secret jail after being there four days (M205). Agustín had apparently gone berserk.

1112 (G. O.) *Manuel Rodríguez Núñez* (as he was known in Spain) and *Manuel Núñez* in Mexico City. Born Casteloblanco, Port., the wandering son of *Francisco Rodríguez*, relaxed, and of *Beatriz Núñez*. He was reconciled April 1646.

1113 *Isabel Texoso* (M. spells Tejoso). Reconciled April 1646. She was a young woman, either a baker (G. O.) or the sister of a baker (M.) in *Veracruz*. (M. never mentions the name of the sister. It may be presumed that she was *Clara Texoso*.) She was the daughter of *Pedro Gomez Texoso* and *Violante Rodríguez*. She liked to read of the lives of the Patriarchs and the prophets of the old Law and used to adjust the Catholic prayers to the Jewish manner, leaving in the names of Jesus and Mary.

1114 *Violante Texoso*. Born Lima, *Peru;* resided in New *Vera Cruz;* seamstress and legitimate daughter of *Rafael Gómez*, merchant, deceased, of Mexico City. Reconciled 1646.

1115 *Manuel Antunez*. Born Mexico City, son of *Diego Antunes* (Port.) merchant and of *Isabel Duarte* alias *de Antunes*, reconciled Jewess. Reconciled April 1646 with sambenito.

1116 *Isabel Duarte*. Born Seville and called *La Antúnez* (M.). (G. O. states she is a *jugadora*, gambler. This is doubted in view of M's statement about her fasts and charity.) She was the daughter of *Marcos Rodríguez Tristán* and *Anna Enriquez*. She was reconciled April 1646. Anna Enríquez was dead but was burned in effigy in the Grand Auto of April 11, 1649. (Comment: The paragraph on *Isabel Duarte* in M. was written by Julio Jiménez Rueda, as part of his additional notes. Pages 113 and 114 provide evidence that a non-Jew cannot fully understand Jewish customs and ritual and cannot distinguish between superstition and fundamentals of religion, psalms, and incantations.)

1117 *Francisco Núñez Navarro*. Born Villa de Chachin, Port.; reside New Galicia (near Michoacan). Bachelor, mendicant merchant, 43 years old. Descendant of new Christians, reconciled 1646.

1118 (G. O.) *Leonor Núñez*. Born Seville. Resident of *New Veracruz,* widow of *Manuel Coronel* (broker in *Veracruz*), legitimate daughter of *Gaspar de Agart* and *Maria Núñez;* reconciled 1646. In M. (p.205) appears that *Manuel Coronel* was burned in effigy in the Grand Auto of 1649 as a fugitive and for being a Jew. The names of this Leonor's parents do not appear in M. or in the *Indice del Ramo de Inquisicion.*

1119 (G. O.) *Luis Muños Pérez*. Born Samamedo, near Lisbon. Peanut dealer, son of *Manuel de Abeña* and *Batola Días Silba;* new Hebrew Christian, reconciled 1646.

1120 *Francisco Gomez Texoso*. Bachelor, merchant, but had previously earned the title of Captain. Born in Valencia, lived in *New Veracruz*. Reconciled 1646. He received the name of Tristán Manuel at his baptism "because he would live sad days because he was baptized through fear." His descendants used the name Tristán for their family name.

1121 *Francisca Texoso.* Maiden, born Seville, resident *New Veracruz.* Baker, reconciled 1646. She confessed, very rebelliously, to being a Jew. In order to have the bread which she and her brother kneaded come out white and tasty, they kneaded it first with water which they used to wash certain obscene parts and then made some circles and Jewish rites in the form of prayers over the dough.

1122 *Margarita de Rivera.* Born Seville, daughter of *Diego Lopez* (merchant, Port.) and of *Blanca de Rivera.* "She was like a witch; her trade was making fancy bows and metal hoops for pregnant women to wear under their skirts. She married *Miguel de Huerta* according to Jewish custom. She was extremely ceremonious and would be in the shrouds and would wash the bodies of Jews and Jewesses, etc." Her mother, known as *Blanca Méndez* in Spain, was 54 years old when she was imprisoned in 1642 and was reconciled with all the members of her family as heretical judaizantes in 1646. She was the widow of *Diego López Rivera,* merchant in Casteloblanco, Port., and the daughter of *Enríque Rios. Obregón,* of Llerena in Estremadura; shipper of Negroes from Angola to New Spain. Both mother and daughter played great roles in the Inquisitorial proceedings from 1642 to 1649. (See Genaro García and M. 115, 191, 193.) It appears that the difficulties for Blanca and her daughters *Margarita, Clara* and *Isabel* and her grandsons *Rafael* and *Gabriel de Granada* began because of the accusation that some of the women had beaten an image of Christ. Gabriel was not quite 14 when arrested. Clara's husband was *Felipe López de Norona.*

1123 *Gaspar Vaez Sevilla.* Bachelor, born Mexico City, son of *Simón Vaez Sevilla* alias *Soburto* and of *Juana Enríquez,* Jews, as were all their ancestors who were relaxed. He was reconciled in 1646 although he had perjured himself and acted badly. When his mother was pregnant with him, the Jews thought that she would bear the Messiah who would be their liberator. Gaspar was a descendant of the tribe of Levi. He was 22 years of age. His father *Simón* was reconciled in the Grand Auto of 1649 with sambenito and confiscation of all his property. Simón was the richest man in the procession at the Auto. P. Bocanegra wrote that he possessed a majestic grandeur and treated other Jews with splendor when they came to his house. He received Jews with recommendations from Liorna, Pisa, Spain and other parts of the world. His credit was such that he could deal in diamonds and from "sackcloth to brocades." *Juana* was reconciled with her husband. She went out to the auto with green candles in her hands and a halter about her neck (the same as other prisoners) but she was condemned to be exiled, perpetual jail unpardonable and 200 lashes. She was a sister of *Isabel Tinoco* who was in the same auto.

1124 *Thomas Núñez de Peralta.* Merchant, born Cubillana, Port., reconciled 1646, the son of *Jorge Baez Alcaiceria,* leather tanner; married to the Jewess *Beatriz Enríquez.* He was related to many Jews in Mexico City and was in charge of those in jail and he induced them not to confess in spite of the fact that the Pope and the King were to send a general pardon because they did not desire that families as large and as important as that of *Núñez de Peralta* and *Simón Vaez de Sevilla* go out in an auto. The Jews of Seville had contributed a great amount of money for him. (Note: Núñez Peralta's father's name is Baez, so spelled by G. O., but others spell it Vaez. This may evidence a relationship with Simón Vaez.)

1125 *Gabriel de Granada.* Son of *Gabriel de Granados* (deceased) and *María Rivera* and grandson of *Blanca Rivera* (as per G. O.) and brother of *Rafael.* (M. states he was 18 years of age but the *proceso* itself states that he was between 13 and 14 years of age. David Fergusson declares that Gabriel was the son of *Manuel de Granada* and of *María de Rivera.* (PAJHS, Vol. 7, 1889, and entry 397.)

1126 *Pedro López de Morales.* Born Rodrigo, Castille; miner and resident of City of *Istan.* Reconciled Jan. 23, 1647. He reported to the Tribunal the money that he had which belonged to other Jews. His daughter was a mestizo and he wanted to take her to Spain so that his family could teach her the Law of Moses. Further information about synagogue vestments and synagogues in Europe, M. 117.

1127 *Francisco León de Xaramillo.* Son of *Duarte de Léon Xaramillo* and of *Isabel Núñez*, reconciled 1647. (M. spells last name with "J" instead of "X".) He was in two procesos because in his first he had concealed some things relative to Judaism concerning himself and his accomplices.

1128 (G. O. only) *Julio Méndez.* Born Villa Visiosa, Port., merchant in Mexico City, descendant of new Hebrew Christians; heretical Jews. Reconciled 1647.

1129 *Manuel Alvarez de Arellano.* Born Jelbes, Port., bachelor. Reconciled 1647. He served as the Jewish mortician and helped the Jews observe all the rites for burial.

1130 *Rodrígo Fernández Correa.* Bachiller, doctor, born in *Veracruz* and brother of *Beatriz Henriquez* and son of *Fernándo Rodríguez.* Beatriz's husband was *Tomás Méndez.* They were all reconciled in the auto of Jan. 23, 1647.

1131 *Miguel Tinoco.* Bachelor, apprentice to silversmith; born Mexico City, son of *Diego Tinoco* (Port.) and *Catalina Enríquez* of Seville. Reconciled April 16, 1646. (G. O. 1647.)

1132 *Juana Tinoco.* Born in Mexico City, wife of *Simón Juárez de Espinosa* (G. O. spells Xuárez) who was a small merchant or storekeeper. She was a descendant of new Hebrew Christians and was reconciled in 1646 (per M.), 1647 (per G. O.). Jiménez Rueda implies that she was a conjurer or familiar with witchcraft and he set forth a lengthy poem (M. p.114) which was recited, and her husband thus was converted to being a Jew. (Note: Jiménez Rueda relies for much of his sources on Genaro García's work, previously cited.)

1133 *Duarte Rodríguez.* Born in Estopedrina, Port., merchant in *New Veracruz*, husband of *Clara Texoso* and descendant of new Christians. Reconciled Jan. 23, 1647. He used to read *Flos Sanctorum* of Villegas and the lives of the patriarchs and prophets, Judith and Esther, and they used to be discussed in his house, which was the central meeting place of the Jews in *Vera Cruz.*

1134 *Diego Rodríguez Arias.* Son of father with same name (G. O. says father was *Antonio Rodríguez Arias*) and *Blanca Enríquez.* He was termed a grand *dogmatist.* (G. O. p.701 says Juana was daughter of *"rabinos dogmatistas"* meaning Antonio and Blanca). He was a bachelor and was born in Seville. He was reconciled in the auto of March 30, 1648 "de vehementi with confiscation of all goods."

1135 *Rafaela Enríquez* (also spelled Henriquez). Born in Seville, married to *Gaspar Juárez* and she was the daughter of *Antonio Rios. Arias* and *Blanca Enriquez.* Reconciled auto of March 30, 1648 "de vehementi with confiscation of all goods." She and her sister, *Micaela Henriquez*, are referred to in the letter of the Inquisitor Dr. don Juan Sáenz de Mañozca dated Nov. 30, 1646 (Archivo de Simancas, Inq. de México, Libro 768 fol. 333).

1136 *Beatriz Enríquez.* Born in Mexico City, daughter of Antonio Rodríguez and Doña *Blanca Enríquez, rabinos* (rabbis) (per G. O. p.699) and wife of *Thomas Núñez de Peralta.* Reconciled March 30, 1648. [She is not to be confused with the earlier *Beatriz Enríquez*, who went to the stake in the famous auto of 1596.] She was 20 years of age and had been taught by her mother how to participate in all the secret Jewish practices, including the ceremonies at and after the funeral, including the eating of a cold, hardboiled egg without salt. Many of the practices are set forth. She was abjured "de vehementi with confiscation of all property."

1137 *Gaspar Juárez.* Father of *Blanca Juarez* (Xuárez per G. O.) and father-in-law of *Jorge Jacinto Bazán* and husband of *Rafaela Enríquez.* He died in jail and was reconciled in effigy with confiscation of goods because he was a Jewish observer of the Law of Moses. *Blanca* was reconciled March 30, 1648 de vehementi and with confiscation of goods. *Jorge Jacinto Bazán* had come to Mexico with great recommendations. He had been in Pisa, Liorna, Salonica, and came from Marseilles to Mexico. Because he was famous, the kin of Simón Baez de Sevilla arranged his wedding with the great beauty, Blanca Juárez. (Interesting exchange of repartee.)

1138   *Leonor Martinez*. She was 14 years at her auto. She was named after her paternal grandmother, *Leonor Martínez de Villa Gómez*, burned in effigy by the Inquisition in Valladolid. She lived in *Guadalajara* with her parents and was reconciled "de vehementi and with confiscation of goods," March 30, 1648. Also reconciled with same punishment was her brother, *Rafael de Sobremonte*, two of the five living children of their famous parents.

1139   *Violante Juárez*. Born *Lima*, Peru; married to *Manuel de Mella* and they lived in *Guadalajara*. Their home was used as the synagogue for the Jews in that city. They were reconciled together in the auto of March 30, 1648, de vehementi and confiscation of all property. *Manuel de Mella* was born in Villa de Guelba, was a goldsmith, son of *Gregorio de Mella*, who had been born in Zamora. Gregorio was a merchant and lived in Malaga and his wife (Manuel's mother) was *Violante Rodríguez*. Both his parents were new Hebrew Christians.

1140   *Elena de Silva* alias *Elena López*. Born Casteloblanco, Port., daughter of *Gaspar Voncalvos Soburto*, an innkeeper and butcher, and of *Leonor Baez*, heretical Jews. She was reconciled April 11, 1649 (G. O. 1648). (Note the name Soburto, that of her paternal grandmother, and Baez, her mother's maiden name. Simón Vaez Sevilla had an alias *Soburto*. It would appear to be a sound deduction that Elena de Silva was related to *Simón Vaez*. G. O. p.700; *Simón* was son of *Gaspar González Soburto*, butcher and innkeeper and was an executioner [verdugo].)

1141   *Pedro de Espinosa*. M. puts him in the auto of April 16, 1646 (de vehementi and confiscation of property), and in that of Jan. 23, 1647. It may be that there were two men with identical names, a not too infrequent occurrence. M. and G. O. write of *Pedro de Espinosa* who was the administrator of the butcher shops in *Sayula*. He was accustomed to read the book *The Mirror of Consolation*, which treated of the patriarchs and prophets of the Old Law. He was married to Doña *Isabel Silva de Enríquez*. He was the son of *Simón Rodríguez* (reconciled) and *Bernardina de Espinosa*. G. O. says he was reconciled in 1649.

1142   *Inés Pereira*. Born in *Esmiquipan*, wife of *Baltazar Díaz Santillan*. Her parents were Portuguese. Baltasar and Inéz were formally abjured, reconciled with sambenitos and confiscation of goods as Jews observing the Law of Moses in the auto of April 11, 1649. (G. O. states she was relaxed in person.)

1143   *Duarte Castaño*. Born Brabantes, Port.; resided in *Caracas;* son of new Hebrew Christians and husband of *Antonio de Silba*, born near Seville. He was reconciled with formal abjuration, sambenito and confiscation of goods April 1649.

1144   *Jorge Duarte* alias *Jorge León*. Born in Mexico City, bachelor and son of de Duarte, relaxed, and of *Isabel Núñez*, related to "reconciliados." Jorge was reconciled in 1649 with sambenito and confiscation of goods. During the ceremonies on the day preceeding the Grand Auto of 1649, *Isabel* requested an audience at 9 P.M. which lasted more than an hour and another at 3 A.M. As a result of these audiences, her departure as well as that of *Leonor Vaez*, the wife of another criminal also condemned to be relaxed, were suspended for the Grand Auto. She and Leonor Vaez (Port.) were reconciled on April 21, 1649, in the Church of Santo Domingo with sambenitos, perpetual jail unpardonable for being Jews. The two women had won a 10-day delay after the Grand Auto and were not relaxed but they did each receive 200 lashes plus the other punishments.

1145   *Francisco López Blandon*, alias *Terrasas*. Bachelor born in Mexico City, a guilder; son of relaxed parents and he was relaxed in person in 1649. He was 31 years of age. He had been in the auto of April 2, 1635, and was therefore a "relapso." He was the son of *Leonor Núñez*, of Madrid, who had been denounced in *Peru* for being an observer of the Law of Moses. In the 1635 auto, he went in a yellow sackcloth garment with a cross of Saint Andrew of red cloth on it. His mother had been 64 years of age in the auto of 1635.

1146 *Juan Méndez Villaviciosa.* Reconciled Jan. 23, 1647. He proclaimed that the Law of Moses was for and should be observed by the whole world and all those who did should dress in red and be very happy, closing it with a great feast. (This last clause may refer to the Jewish custom of terminating a course of study with a party known in Hebrew as a *siyum.*)

1147 *Juan Méndes.* Born San Vicente Davera (Port.), merchant. He died in *Texcoco* and was the husband of *Ana Gomez* of Chaves. He was the son of new Hebrew Christians and was burned in effigy in 1649. M. gives date of March 29, 1648 and that he was "abjured de levi" for observing the Law of Moses.

1148 *Francisco de Amezquito* (G. O. omits the capital A). Bachelor; born in Segovia, Castille. Merchant; son of new Hebrew Christians; deceased. Burned in effigy 1649.

1149 *Diego de Campos Segovia.* Port.; merchant from *Campeche* to *Veracruz*, son of new Hebrew Christians. Burned in effigy 1649.

1150 *Juana Rodríguez* (G. O. says "alias de los Angeles") born Lisbon, Port.; wife of *Diego Núñez Batoca* (he was reconciled). She was the daughter of new Hebrew Christians and died prior to 1649 and was burned in effigy together with four of her children; all at the same time in the Grand Auto of 1649. She was the mother of Doña *Blanca Enríquez* noted as "famous *dogmatist,*" *rabina* (female rabbi, but *rebbitzin,* the wife of a rabbi, might be closer to the truth). Blanca was a *relapso* having been imprisoned earlier and having confessed under torture.

1151 *Justa Méndez.* Born in Seville, died in Mexico City prior to 1649. Daughter of *Francisco Méndes* (Port.) and of *Clara Enríquez.* She had been reconciled and was burned in effigy in 1649. At 20 years of age, she was called the "beautiful" and had a genteel demeanor. She was a seamstress. After her first reconciliation at beginning of seventeenth century, she married *Francisco Núñez* and secured permission by letter of June 4, 1608, from the Patriarch of the Indies and the Inquisitor General "to wear silk and fine linens, gold, silver and precious stones." (This is most remarkable because she had been in the auto of 1596 and was condemned to wear sambenito and to perpetual jail M.124.)

1152 *Luis Pérez Roldán.* Born in Mexico. Husband of *Isabel Núñez*, relaxed, and son, cousin and uncle of various reconciled and relaxed. He was reconciled in 1649 with 200 lashes and sambenito. (M. has him burned in effigy in 1649, but in view of his appearance, per M. in the auto of Nov. 19, 1659, there is an obvious error.) He was a fencing instructor. In 1649, he was condemned to 100 lashes and permanent sambenito to be worn over his clothes because he did not comply with his former punishment. During his imprisonment he explained that he did not wear his sambenito when he went to sell skeins of *agave* or to give fencing lessons, because nobody would have anything to do with him otherwise. He was kept in jail until the first opportunity to banish him from Mexico.

1153 *Pedro Tinoco.* Possessed degree of Bachiller in medicine. He was a *doctor,* single, and born in Mexico City, son of *Diego Tinoco* and *Catalina Silva* alias *Enríquez* (both parents relaxed) and descendant of other equal heretics. He was reconciled in 1649. P. Bocanegra reports that "*Pedro* and *Isabel Tinoco* and his sister *Juana Enríquez* while in the cupola with the insigna of relajados, joined their hands and with tears in their eyes" they entreated for an audience which was granted to them. He only wanted mercy. He refused to convert.

1154 (G. O. only) *Francisca Núñez.* Born Mexico City, deceased; daughter of *Justa Méndez*, relaxed, and *Francisco Núñez* alias Rodríguez. Burned in effigy 1649.

1155 *Francisco Botello.* Resident *Tacubaya.* He was descendant of new Christians on his mother's side, who were relaxed. He was reconciled for heretical judaizante, then relapsed and was relaxed in person in 1649 (G. O.). M. says he was abjured *de vehementi,* for suspicion of being a Jew, in the Grand Auto of 1649. His wife, *María de Zarate,* was imprisoned for the crime of being a Jew and was in the auto of November 1659 when Francisco was relaxed in person. There is a graphic description of the torture administered to him (in fact five turns of the wheel. He stayed in the hospital four years to cure his illness resulting from the torture.) He was burned alive and was termed, by the S. O., one of the most obdurate Jews in many centuries that has been punished; this, because "he would not mention by name Jesus nor the Holy Virgin, his mother." (Note errors of G. O. and M.)

1156 *Leonor Vaez Sevilla.* Maiden, born and died in Mexico City, daughter of *Simón Vaez Sevilla* alias Soburto and of *Juana Enríquez,* his wife. She was burned in effigy in 1649 for heretical judaizante.

1157 *Gonzálo Flores* alias *Gonzálo Vaez Méndez.* His Jewish name was Samuel; born La Torre de Moncorbo, Port.; merchant and trader in the provinces; son of new Hebrew Christians; he feigned insanity while in jail and was relaxed in person in Grand Auto of 1649 because he was impenitent. For three years he had denied being a Jew, then confessed to being an observer of the Law of Moses. Five months later, he retracted his confession. Two years later he was examined by doctors, surgeons and nurses of the Hospital for the Insane and all declared him sane.

1158 *Ana López de Chavez.* Born Burgo de Osma, Castille; resident of *Puebla* where she died; daughter of *Isabel Alvarez,* new Christian; wife of *Juan Gómez* relaxed; burned in effigy in 1649.

1159 *Ana de León Carvajal.* She was the daughter of *Francisco Rodríguez Matos* and *Francisca Núñez de Carvajal.* She had been born in Medina del Campo, Port., and was the widow of *Cristobal Miguel* a merchant. Both her parents had been relaxed. She was the only one cited in the procesos who had been reconciled in the general auto of 1601. In 1649, she was 66 years of age, sick with cancer of the breast and confined to lying on her back because of this and other serious ailments.

1160 *Juan de Araujo* (spelled Arango in G. O.). He was Portuguese. He died in *Caracas;* he was a dealer in Negroes. He died crushed in the ruins of a church and was burned in effigy in 1649.

1161 *Tomás Trevino de Sobremonte* (name also spelled Tremiño alias *Gerónimo de Represa;* born Medina de Rioseco, Castille; married to *María Gómez (relaxada);* son, cousin and uncle of many reconciliados; relapso and burned alive 1649. According to M. he was reconciled in the auto of June 15, 1625, together with *Antonio Vaez Casteloblanco* or *Tirado* and both appear in the auto of April 11, 1649. Treviño declared that he wanted to observe the Law of Moses till his death. Since his proceso and his final words have been repeated innumerable times, no further space will be devoted to his end. He had fasted for five years while in prison. (Note: Fasting sometimes meant refraining from eating from sunrise to sunset.)

1162 *Mayor López.* Port., wife of *Francisco Blandón López.* Both were old Hebrew Christians. She was dead but burned in effigy in 1649.

1163 *Pedro de Mercado.* Son of *Dr. Mercado,* Medico (per G. O.), of the Court of His Majesty; heretical Jewish fugitive; burned in effigy 1649. M. states that he was a man of letters and it would seem that he became involved because at a performance of a comedy that he wrote he gave the first seats to two Jews who had been reconciled by the S. O. "while many Catholic and honored people were standing" and later took the Jews to his home and feted them.

1164 *Simón Montero*. Married Doña *Elena Montero* in Seville, the daughter of new Hebrew Christians. He feigned repentance and confession. He had been imprisoned in 1635 because he had wanted to buy a "virginal" statue for a friend from the Abess of a Convent in Mexico. The S. O. had wanted to first put him to torture, but they let him free in 1635. He used to travel between Seville and Mexico. He went mad in prison but in spite of that, he was relaxed in person in 1649.

1165 (G. O.) *María Rivera*. Born Seville, wife of *Manuel Granado* or *Granados*, daughter, sister, aunt and cousin of many *relaxados*. She was burned in effigy with her bones in 1649 as heretical Jewess.

1166 *Julian de Arboláez* (G. O.: *Arboles*). Born Amsterdam, Holland, descendant of Portuguese; resided in *Chamacuero, Michoacan;* bachelor. (There are a series of names in G. O. which may indicate a relationship to Treviño.) Burned in effigy 1649.

1167 (G. O.) *Manuel López*. Born Vallona in Galicia, reside *Vera Cruz*, broker; married to *Leonor Núñez*, a reconciliada. He was burned in effigy in 1649, although dead.

1168 (G. O.) *Sebastian Ramón*. Born Seville, merchant or peddlar, died in *San Juan de los Llanos;* burned in effigy 1649.

1169 *Isabel Tinoco*. Born *Zacatecas*, resided *Mexico City*, wife of *Manuel de Acosta* alias *Francisco de Torres;* reconciled daughter of *Diego Tinoco* and *Isabel Silva (relaxados)*. She was reconciled in 1649 as heretical Jewess.

1170 (G. O.) *Isabel de Silva* alias *Correa*. Born Casteloblanco, Port., married to *Antonio Carabajal*, daughter of reconciliados; reconciled 1649.

1171 (G. O.) *Rodrigo Fernández Salseda*. Husband of *Inéz López* who was born in Seville and was his widow. She was the mother of reconciliados and grandmother of *relaxados*. She was burned in effigy in 1649.

1172 *Diego Rodríguez* (G. O. alias or *Bandejo*) Port., of caste of new Hebrew Christians; fugitive, burned in effigy 1649.

1173 *Pedro López Núñez*. Born Seville, merchant, resided in *Manila;* brother of *Isabel Tristan*. Burned in effigy 1649.

1174 *Gonzálo Vaez*. Born Cateloblanco, resident *Cuyuacan* (this differs from Indice of AGN), merchant, son of new Hebrew Christians. He had been in the secret cells of the S. O. in October 1627 for opening letters to the S. O., but he did not confess even in the torture rack and was released. In 1649, after an examination attesting his sanity, he was relaxed in person in the Grand Auto. He was an uncle, nephew and cousin of other penitents in the same auto.

1175 (G. O. & AGN) *Manuel de León*. Born San Martín de la Vega (near Toledo), traveling merchant; son of reconciliados and penitents. Reconciled as heretical judaizante 1678.

1176 *Juan Langourán*. Born Bordeaux, accused of Lutheranism and Judaism. He was reconciled in person Aug. 9, 1795. It was for his Judaism that he was found guilty.

1177 (M. only) *Jorge Ramírez de Montilla*. Reconciled in the auto of April 16, 1646 for being a Jew.

1178 (M. & AGN) *Melchor Rodríguez López*. Abjured *de vehementi* for observing the Law of Moses, in the auto of March 30, 1648.

1179 (M. only) *Luis de Tejoso*. Reconciled with sambenitos for being a Jew, in the auto of April 16, 1646.

1180 (M. only) *Francisco Franco de Morera*. Reconciled as Jew, January 23, 1647.

1181 (M. only) *Pedro Bernal*. Reconciled for observing Law of Moses, March 29, 1648.

1182 (M. only) *Catalina Gómez la Cartuja*. Reconciled for observing Law of Moses, in auto of March 29, 1648. There was also a *Catalina Gómez*.

1183 (M. only) *Gracia Gómez*. Reconciled in auto of March 29, 1648, for observing Law of Moses.

1184 (M.) *Luis González*. Reconciled in auto of March 29, 1648, for observing Law of Moses.

1185 (M.) *Damian de Lucena Baez*. Penitenced for suspicion of the crime of Judaism, in auto of March 1648.

1186 (M.) *Enrique Jorge de Acosta*. Penitenced for suspicion of the crime of Judaism, in auto of March 1648.

1187 (M.) *Leonor Enríquez*. Penitenced for suspicion of the crime of Judaism, in auto of March 1648.

1188 (M.) *Diego Díaz Vaez*. Penitenced for suspicion of the crime of Judaism, in auto of March 1648.

1189 (M.) *Felipa Núñez de la Paz*. Penitenced for suspicion of the crime of Judaism, in auto of March 1648.

1190 (M.) *Diego Fernández de Elvas*. Burned in effigy as a Jew in the auto of March 30, 1649, with his bones, which were disinterred from the grave. He had died in jail.

1191 (M.) *Isabel de la Cruz*. Burned in effigy as a Jew in the auto of March 30, 1649, with her bones, which were disinterred from the grave. She had died in jail.

1192 (M.) *Simón Rodríguez Núñez*. Relaxed in person in auto of March 29, 1648. He was Portuguese, had lived in Seville; was a *relapso* in Judaism.

1193 (M.) *Beatriz Núñez*, wife of Diego de Ocaña, who was reconciled in 1528.

1194 (M.) *Leonor Xuárez de Ocana*. Daughter of Diego de Ocaña, who was reconciled in 1528.

1195 (M.) *García Xuárez*. Son of Diego de Ocaña (see 1194).

1196 (M.) *Diego de Ocaña*. Grandson of Diego de Ocaña (see 1194).

1197 (M.) *Guiomar de Rivera*. Daughter of *Miguel Núñez*, wife of *Luis de Carbajal*, el viejo, the Governor.

1198 (M.) *Miguel Núñez*. Father-in-law of *Luis de Carbajal*, el viejo, the Governor, who was a broker in the traffic of Negroes in Santo Domingo for the King of Portugal.

1199 (M.) *Enrique Rodríguez Obregón*. Father of *Blanca Méndez*, as she was called in Spain, and doña *Blanca de Rivera* in Mexico. He came from Llerena in Extremadura and was a broker of Negroes from Angola to New Spain.

1200 (M.) *Antonio Núñez*. Brother of *Ana Núñez* and *Francisco de León*. (There is an interesting report on customs which took place on a Friday and "a new invention of circumcision.")

1201 (M.) *Jorge Espinosa* alias *Jorge Serrano*. He was sentenced to 200 lashes, service in the galleys and exile to Spain 1639 by the Inquisition at *Lima*. He escaped to Mexico, assumed his alias and became *alcalde mayor* (chief constable) of *Cuazualco*. He was rearrested and was in the Inquisition jail after 1649.

Appendix C

Sundry Documents

Mention was made in the Introduction that not all the Mexican Inquisition Documents are in the Archivo General de la Nación. Men such as G. R. G. Conway purchased many and made transcripts of others. These men in turn sold or donated originals and copies to various institutions, universities, and libraries. The beneficiaries range from the Politechnico Instituto at Monterrey, Mexico, to the University of Aberdeen, Scotland. They are to be found in the Library of Congress, Washington, D.C., and at the American Jewish Historical Society in New York City.

The purchase and sale of original Mexican historical papers had been a lucrative trade. It even induced some people to steal some from the AGN and others to smuggle them out of Mexico and to violate criminal laws. It is believed that Padre Fisher, personal priest of Emperor Maximilian, shipped many to France and the Vatican.

There is a legend that General Francisco (Pancho) Villa used many thousands of documents that he had removed from the churches in Querétaro and San Luis Potosí to make a victory bonfire. This was during the Revolution (1912-1917), and he did not appreciate their historical value. Others were destroyed by fire, as appears from the account of Col. David Fergusson in the footnote to Item 297 of this Index.

About 1906, E. Nott Anable of New York was peddling Inquisition documents (see correspondence with Henry C. Lea at the Lea Memorial Library, University of Pennsylvania). He had at least thirty-one volumes of documents which ranged between the years 1601 to 1692. They are superficially described by Elkan N. Adler in his *Auto de Fe and Jew* (pp. 156-162). It may be that the documents in the Huntington Library, discussed in the next paragraph, are part of the Anable papers. There is a duplication of names and a repetition of the order in which they appear in Adler's description cited above.

William Blake was a dealer in manuscripts and old books in Mexico City. In 1907, he sold many volumes of original documents for $1,500 to a Walter Douglas of Arizona. These documents, comprising forty-seven volumes, were later presented by Walter Douglas to the Henry E. Huntington Library, San Marino, California. This list has not heretofore been published. They appear in this Appendix in the same manner as set forth in the List supplied by the Library to the AGN. Particular mention must be made of Volumes 1 and 2, which are indispensable for research on the Mexican Colonial Era. With the exception of Volume 41, Alexandro Suarez, all the documents pertaining to Jews are actually only fragments of the total *proceso* of the individuals involved.

Prof. Ivie E. Cadenhead, Jr., compiled *The G. R. G. Conway Collection in the Gilcrease Institute: A Checklist,* which revealed the location of many documents. Prof. Cadenhead graciously supplied the extracts from his notes, which have been added to the material taken from his article. Again we find that the documents are only fragments of the total testimony, the major portions of which, in some instances, are in the AGN.

There are a few documents in the Henry C. Lea Memorial Library at the University of Pennsylvania. Dr. Kenneth E. Setton, the curator, has presented microfilms thereof to the AGN. Others are at the University of Texas; the Historical Manuscripts Commission of London; the Thomas E. Gilcrease Institute of Tulsa, Oklahoma; Washington State University, Pullman, Washington; one at the Jewish Theological Seminary, New York City; and some at Trinity College, Dublin, Ireland. There is no complete record of their various locations.

We have left for last the Archives of Spain. It is known that José Toribio Medina did much research at the Archives of Simancas and in the Archives of the Indies. We are indebted in more ways than one to Don J. Ignacio Rubio Mañé, Director of AGN, who has stated that important information pertaining to Mexican Jewry is to be found in the section on Encomiendas in the Archives of the Indies.

This Appendix will list those of Jews or of Jewish interest that are capable of adequate description. To facilitate location, the following abbreviations will be employed:

G = Thomas Gilcrease Institute, Tulsa, Oklahoma
A = Anable (location unknown)
H = Henry E. Huntington Library, San Marino, California
L = Henry C. Lea Memorial Library, University of Pennsylvania, Philadelphia, Pennsylvania
J.T.S. = Jewish Theological Seminary, New York City
W.S.U. = Washington State University, Pullman, Washington

The enumeration is a continuation of the previous appendices. The aforesaid abbreviations in parentheses follow the number. Wording follows the original publication or correspondence. The list does not follow the alphabetical order of abbreviations.

1201 (A) *Leonor de Caceres* (1601). Only child of *Antonio Diaz de Caceres and Catalina Cueva de Carbajal*. Proceso against her, her mother, and her sisters for Judaism.

1202 (A) *Francisco de Carbajal* (1602).

1203 (A) *Domingo Diaz*, alias *Domingo Rodríguez*. Portuguese, resided in *Puebla*, 1622. Charge of Judaism.

1204 (A) *Baltazar del Valle*, alias *Diaz*. Portuguese, Judaism, 1624 and 1634; born Zamora; 46 years of age in 1634; peddler; married and lived in *Pachuca*.

1205 (A) *Isabel Texoso* (1642). 60 years old; a Jewess. In 1659, the Fiscal of the Santo Oficio brought a proceso against her memory and fame.

1206 (A) *Simon López* (1642). Born Guarda, Port.; peddler; follower of the Laws of Moses. Among these papers were also advices that *Juan Duarte, Francisco López*, and *Simon López* had been imprisoned and advices about letters from López while he was in the Inquisition prison.

1207 (A) *George Jacinto* (1642). Following the Law of Moses; husband of *Blanca Juarez*. Thirty-eight witnesses testified against him and he gave evidence against 33. This case was tried before the celebrated "Manozca."

1208 (A) *Diego Juarez* (1642). From *Patzcuaro*, Michoacán; born Lisbon; 43 years old; 55 witnesses. This proceso has 300 pages.

1209 (A) *Miss Francisco Texoso*. Of *Veracruz* (1642); born Seville; 30 years old; a Jewess; 27 witnesses against her and she testified against 42; "the celebrated Irishman Azuzena had criminal connexion with her as she had with many other persons."

1210 (A) *George Montoya* (1642). Born Casteloblanco, Port.; a fugitive; a Jew; he was also a prisoner of the Inquisition in Goa.

1211 (A) *Antonio Tinoco* (1642). Deceased; son of *James Tinoco*, deceased, and Mrs. *Henriqueta* of Mexico; following Law of Moses. Letters and advices to his sons and descendants, grandchildren, heirs, etc.

1212 (A) *Catalina Enríquez* (1643). Of *Veracruz;* Jewess following the Law of Moses; 30 years old; born Seville; widow of *Pedro Arias Maldonado*, Port.; she has 22 brothers and 90 persons gave evidence against her.

1213 (A) *Gaspar de Fonseca*. Dead; resident *Ayula;* criminal cause for being a Jew.

1214 (A) *Francisco Rasen*. A Frenchman from Normandy; a Jew, Calvinist, and Lutheran (1643). 90 testified against him.

1215 (A) *Margarita Morena* (1643). Wife of *Amaro Diaz Martarana*, peddler in Mexico City; aged 32.

a 1216 (A) *De Palavera* (1673). No statement of crime appears in Anable's description. (He lived in Tepeaca where many Jews resided.)

1217 (L) Isabelle Rodríguez. Jewess; wife of Manuel Diaz; born Salceda, Port.; 114 page proceso.

1218 (L) *Manuel Diaz*. Jew; born Fondón, Port.; proceso of 154 pages; he was relaxed to secular arm and his property confiscated.

1219 (L) *Sebastian Rodríguez* (1595), born San Vicente Davera, Jew; sanbenito, perpetual prison, and confiscation of property. Proceso of 178 pages.

1220 (W.S.U.) *Simon de Leon* (1647) aged 15 years; a practicing Jew. His father was *Duarte de Leon Xaramillo* (not to be confused with Duarte de Leon, uncle of Luis de Carvajal, el viejo) was burned in the auto of 1649 and his mother *Isabel Núñez* was reconciled at the last moment. She was to have been burned. (This case is found in annexed Bibliography.)

1221 (W.S.U.) *Luis de la Cruz*. An insignificant slave who belonged to *Inez Pereira*, daughter of *Ana Gómez* who was a first cousin of *Francisco Botello*. This was in 1659. Luis carried messages from the Jewish prisoners in the secret cells of the Inquisition to their families and friends. (Much information is contained in this proceso, cited in annexed Bibliography.)

1222 (J.T.S.) *Juan García*, alias *Juan de Alvarado* (born Mexico City), heresy and apostasy.

1223 (G) *Diego Diez Nieto* (1598-1605), 124 leaves. Testimony of eleven witnesses, and a few related documents. A Portuguese Jew. This is a characteristic case of the later sixteenth century, when trials involving Judaism became prevalent in Mexico.

1224 (G) *Diego López*. Born San Vicente Davera, single and descendant of new Christians. The record of a Portuguese Jew, including the testimony of witnesses and many genealogical documents. He was first sentenced to three years imprisonment (1595) and was accused again (1598) and further punished. 122 leaves.

a 1225 (G) Inquisition, 1624-1632: Relaciones. 318 leaves. This is a register of cases and sentences for this period, with an original index of names. Summaries of about 200 cases are given.

1226 (G) *Simon López*. 191 leaves, 1634-1635. Otherwise known as Marcus del Valle, a Portuguese merchant.

1227 (G) *Clara de Silva*. Proceso and criminal cause, 1642-1649, 28 leaves. The defendant had died at the time judgment was pronounced but she was nevertheless condemned as a Jewess; her goods were confiscated and her memory condemned; her body was disinterred and burned.

1228 (G) *Henrique Fernández*. Proceso and criminal cause, 1642-1649, 230 leaves. A Portuguese Jew and merchant in Guadalajara. His death occurred in prison, before sentence was delivered. The file includes a great many other notices of contemporary inquisitorial records on Mexican Jews.

1229 (G) *Juan Duarte de Espinosa*. Proceso and criminal case, 1642-1650, 82 leaves, against a Portuguese Jew imprisoned in Oaxaca and sent to Mexico. He was sentenced to 100 lashes and perpetual banishment from the Indies, from Seville, and from Madrid.

1230 (G) *Juan Méndez de Villaviciosa*. Proceso and criminal case, 1642-1647, 285 leaves. A Portuguese Jew, sentenced to 200 lashes, five years as a galley slave, and perpetual banishment from the Indies.

1231 (G) *Duarte de Leon Jaramillo*. Third proceso and criminal case, 215 leaves, 1642-1649. Born Casteloblanco. A famous Mexican Jew and many witnesses testified to his Judaism and to his teaching Judaism to his family and others. He was executed in the auto de fe of 1647.

1232 (G) *Duarte Rodríguez*. Proceso and criminal case, 1642-1647, 68 leaves. A Portuguese Jew and merchant in *Veracruz*. After having been sentenced by the Inquisition in *Lima,* he fled to Mexico but was resentenced there for continued Judaism. He was punished with 200 lashes and perpetual banishment from the Indies, Seville, and Madrid.

1233 (G) *Clara Núñez*. Proceso and criminal cause for Judaism, 1647-1648, 72 leaves. She was sentenced to banishment from the Indies, from Seville, and from Madrid.

1234 (G) *Ana Núñez*. Proceso and criminal cause, 1647-1648, 54 leaves. She was the twelve-year-old daughter of *Duarte de Leon Jaramillo* (see 1231 above). Her father was alleged to have removed a portion of her flesh and eaten it in sacrifice. She was sentenced to perpetual banishment from the Indies, Madrid, and Seville.

(W.S.U.) *Ana Núñez*. There is a manuscript (C-42, of the J. Horace Nunemaker Hispanic American Collection of the Archives Library of the Washington State University Libraries) of "100 pages or more" pertaining to her. She is the same child as in 1234 above.

1235 (G) *Simon Payba*. Proceso against his memory and fame. 1597. 59 leaves. A Portuguese Jew; the first half deals with his wife, *Beatriz Enriquez*.

1236 (G) *Juan de Araujo*. Proceso of 21 leaves. 1649. (Believed by compiler to be part of proceso against person of same name who was a Jew.)

a 1237 (H) Vol. 1, List of Inquisition Trials, 1525-1811. The original *borrador* (draft) with entries made from time to time by different secretaries of the Inquisition.

a 1238 (H) Vol. 2, *Abecedario* (alphabetical list) of all prisoners, 1525 to the eighteenth century.

1239 (H) *Leonor Rodríguez*. Trial for Judaism, 634 pp., 1597. Vol. 7.

1240 (H) *Leonor de Caceres*. Trial for being a Jew, 111 pp., 1601. Vol. 11.

1241 (H) *Baltazar del Valle*. Trial for being a Jew, 1634, 146 pp. in Vol. 17 and 369 pp. in Vol. 23.

1242 (H) *Simon López de Aguarda*. Trial for observing the Law of Moses, 1642, 492 pp., Vol. 24.

1243 (H) *Jorge Jacinto*. Trial for observing the Law of Moses, 1642, Vol. 24.

1244 (H) *Francisca Texodo*. Trial for being a Jewess, 1642, Vol. 25.

1245 (H) *Jorge de Montoya*. Trial for being a Jew, 1642. Vol. 25 has 360 pp. covering this trial and 1243 above.

1246 (H) *Diego Juarez de Figueroa*. Trial for being a Jew, 192 pp. in Vol. 26.

1247 (H) *Antonio Tinoco*. Trial for being a Jew. 1643. 102 pp. in Vol. 27.

1248 (H) *Isabel Texosso*. Trial for being a Jewess, 1642-1659, 250 pp. in Vol. 28.

1249 (H) *Catalina Enriquez*. Trial for observing the Law of Moses, 1643, 250 pp. in Vol. 29. These pages include 1250 *infra*.

1250 (H) *Gaspar de Fonseca*. Trial for heresy. Vol. 29.

1251 (H) *Francisco Razin* (Rassan). Trial for heresy, 1643-1653, Vol. 30.

1252 (H) *Margarita Morera*. Trial for being a Jewess. 1643, 200 pp. in Vol. 31.

1253 (H) *Alexandro Suarez de Mesquita*. Trial for Judaism, 1718, 702 pp. in Vol. 41.

Glossary

Abjuración—denial, disavowal or renunciation (*de vehementi*—strong suspicion; *de levi*—light suspicion of heresy).

Acusación—accusation or charge made by any official of the Inquisition.

Auto de fe—literally, Act of Faith. It was a religious procession. There were different kinds: *auto particular* or *autillo,* which was for light offenses and could be private or held within convent grounds without outsiders present; *auto general* or *auto público general,* held as a grand fiesta day, a public holiday being declared and attendance being practically mandatory for all within miles around, including Indians. Not all the penitents at these *autos general* went to the stake. Those who recanted in time recited the most debasing confessions holding a candle in each hand. Decrees for less than capital punishment were read aloud and sambenitos donned.

Comisario—the agents of the Inquisition in the different towns of the kingdom, including all jurisdictions of the Santo Oficio.

Declaración—declaration or deposition made by any witness before the Inquisition.

Denunciación—made by any person other than officials of the Santo Oficio.

Dogmatista—included the meaning of being stubborn in one's faith in addition to being a rabbi or religious leader and even one who indulged in proselytizing activities.

Edict of Faith—an edict read in church that gave heretics an opportunity to secure absolution by making a confession within thirty days after the reading of the document in church. However, many confessants found themselves subsequently imprisoned because they had not revealed the names of their family or friends who had also been heretics. It is safe to assume that the Church entertained the theory that where there was one Jew there were many more and that the Jews knew of the existence of each other.

Familiar—an Inquisition officer devoted primarily to investigations.

Fiscal—prosecutor for the Inquisition.

Gachupin—a person born in Spain. Used principally in Mexico, where they constituted the social aristocracy.

Garrote—the extinguishment of life by the tightening of a cord about the neck (sometimes the temples and skull) of the guilty before they are burned at the stake. This kindness was reserved for those who abjured their heresy after being found guilty (but before leaving the secret jails of the Inquisition) and reaffirmed their faith in Catholicism.

Información—information, charge or accusation.

Judaizante—a Judaizer or one who Judaizes or follows Jewish rites and ritual. This term was applied primarily to those who were Jewish apostates but practiced Judaism secretly. Some had the word "dogmatizer" appended to "judaizante" and these sought to bring back to Judaism the nuevo cristianos (new Christians). See Dogmatista.

Judío—a Jew, Jewish or Judaical.

113

Landrecilla—the cutting away of forbidden fat and veins from the leg of the animal according to Jewish law. The removal was done after the animal had been slaughtered. It is known as "porging" in English.

Proceso—inquisition lawsuits or trials.

Reconciliado—one who was caught straying from the Faith for the first time, confessed the error of his ways and whose sentence or verdict was fixed by the Santo Oficio. He or she was readmitted to the Faith and punishment usually consisted of loss of property and wearing a sambenito.

Relajado—while the term literally means to be relaxed, in the context of Inquisition vocabulary the relajado was to be turned over to the secular arm of the law which was to condemn him to burning at the stake. The Church itself never ordered capital punishment since it wanted no blood on its hands. The act of turning over was "relajacion." The clergy was present at the quemadero (place where prisoners were burned) but only in a spiritual or religious capacity. The prisoner might want to make confession or seek the Church.

Relapso—relapsed; a reversion to criminal or heretical conduct. A person who had been converted and then reverted to his original faith.

Sambenito (also sanbenito)—garments worn by penitent convicts of the Inquisition. There were different kinds (depending on the nature of the punishment or penance). After the completion of the judgment, they were returned to the Santo Oficio and then hung on the walls of the Cathedral with the name of the wearer, the date and details of his crime. In later times, *tablillas* were substituted for the sambenitos on the Cathedral walls.

Bibliography With Annotations

Prior to and Including the Colonial Period

Abbreviations: AGN - Archivo General de la Nación de México
    HAHR - Hispanic American Historical Review
    PAJHS - Publications of the American Jewish Historical Society

BOOKS

Alder, Elkan Nathan. *Auto de Fe and Jew.* London: Henry Frowde, Oxford University Press, 1908.

Albanes, Ricard C. *Los judios a través de los siglos.* México, D.F.: Privately printed, *ca.* 1939.
    The author's name is believed to be a pseudonym. There are anti-Semitic comments on the post-Colonial period.

Allesio Robles, Vito. *Coahuila y Texas en la epoca colonial.* Mexico, D.F.: Editorial Cultura, 1938.

Amador De Los Rios, José. *Historia social politica y religiosa de los judíos de Espana y Portugal.* 2 vols. Madrid: Aguilar, 1960.

Apocrypha, The, or *Non-Canonical Books of the Bible.* The King James Version, edited by Manuel Komroff. New York: Tudor Publishing Co., 1937.

AGN. Documentos del ramo de la inquisición. 1553 vols. and 15 volume *Indice,* 1521 to 1823.

Baer, Yitzhak (Fritz). *A History of the Jews in Christian Spain.* Vol. I. Philadelphia: Jewish Publication Society, 1961.

Baez-Camargo, G. *Protestantes enjuiciados por la inquisicion en Iberoamérica.* México, D.F.: Casa Unida de Publicaciones, 1960.

Barrios, Daniel Levi (Miguel) de. *Luces de la ley divina.* n.p., *ca.* 1660.
    He confused Tomás Treviño de Sobremonte with Francisco Maldonado de Silva of Lima, Peru.

Bernardete, Mair José. *Hispanic Culture and Character of the Sephardic Jews.* New York: Hispanic Institute in the United States, 1953.

Bible, The Pentateuch. Edited by Rabbi J. H. Hertz. London: Geoffrey Cumberledge. Oxford University Press, 1951.

Bocanegra, Mathias de. *Auto general de la fé celebrado por los señores, el Ilmo. y Rmo. don Juan de Manozca, . . . de 11 de abril 1649.* México: Antonio Calderon, 1649.

Braden, Charles S. *Religious Aspects of the Conquest of Mexico.* Durham: Duke University Press, 1930.

Carreño, Alberto Maria. *Don Fray Juan de Zumárraga.* México: Editorial Jus, 1950.

"Carvajal, Luis de (El Mozo), Procesos de." Publicaciones AGN Vol. XXVIII. México: Secretaría de Gobernación, 1953.

Castro, Américo. *The Structure of Spanish History*. Princeton, N.J.: Princeton University Press, 1954.

Catholic Encyclopedia. 15 vols. New York: Robert Appleton & Co., 1907.

Ceram, C. W. *Gods, Graves, and Scholars*. Translated from German by E. B. Garside. New York: Alfred A. Knopf, 1952.

Clavijero, Francisco Javier. *Historia antigua de México*. 2 vols. México.
The author was a Jesuit monk.

Collier, John. *Indians of the Americas*. New York: New American Library, 1951.

Conway, G. R. G. *The G. R. G. Conway Archives*. At the Library of Congress, Washington, D.C.

Cuevas, Mariano. *Historia de la nación mexicana*. México: Talleres Tipografico Modelo, 1940.
The validity of some material is affected by an anti-Semitic and anti-Protestant attitude.

Díaz del Castillo, Bernal. *Historia verdadera de la conquista de la Nueva España*. México: Editorial Porrúa, 1960.
The abridged English edition does not contain the few references to Jews in Mexico.

Enciclopedia Judaica Castellana. 10 vols. México: Editorial Enciclopedia Judaica Castellana, 1948.

Farnsworth, Dewey. *The Americas before Columbus*. Salt Lake City: Deseret Book Co., 1956.

Fisher, Lillian E. *The Background of Revolution for Mexican Independence*. Boston: Christopher Publishing House, 1934.

García, Genaro. *Documentos inéditos ó muy raros de la historia mexicana*. Vols. 5 and 28. Mexico: Librería de la viuda de Ch. Bouret, 1910.
Vol. 5 was printed *ca*. 1906 as *La inquisición de México*, and Vol. 28 is known as *Autos de fé de la inquisición de México*, 1646-1648.

García Gutiérrez, P. *La poesia religiosa en México*. México, D.F.: n.n., 1917.

García Icazbalceta, Joaquin. *Bibliografía mexicana del siglo XVI*. México: Fondo de Cultura Económica, 1954.
This new edition has corrections and addenda by Agustin Millares Carlo. It also has an Index and is a vast improvement over the 1886 edition.

González Obregón, Luis. *Mexico viejo: Noticias históricas, tradiciones, leyendas y costumbres*. Mexico: Editorial Patria, 1959.
This is a new edition with corrections and additions. The original was published in 1895.

Greenleaf, Richard E. *Zumárraga and the Mexican Inquisition*. Washington, D.C.: Academy of Franciscan History, 1962.

Gruening, Ernest D. *Mexico and Its Heritage*. New York: D. Appleton-Century Co., 1942.

Guijo, Gregorio Martín de. *Diario de Guijo, años de 1648-1654*. México: Editorial Porrúa, 1952.

Hay, Malcolm. *Europe and the Jews*. Introduction by Thomas Sugrue and New Preface by Walter Kaufman. Boston: Beacon Press, 1960.

Hilton, Ronald. *Handbook of Hispanic Source Materials and Research Organization in the U.S.* 2d ed. Stanford and Los Angeles: Stanford University Press, 1956.

Ibáñez, Mariel Yolanda. *La inquisición en México durante el siglo SVI*. Mexico: Imprenta Universitaria, 1946.

Jacobs, Joseph. *An Inquiry into the Sources of the History of the Jews in Spain*. New York: Macmillan & Co., 1894.
This book is an excellent guide to the Archives in Spain where are housed Inquisition documents pertaining to Jews.

Jewish Encyclopedia. 12 vols. New York and London: Funk & Wagnalls Co., 1901-1907.

Jiménez Rueda, Julio. *Herejías y superstitiones en la Nueva España: Los heterodoxos en México*. México: Imprenta Universitaria, 1946.

Kayserling, M. *Sephardim; Romanische Poesien der Jüden in Spanien*. Leipzig: n.n., 1859.

Lea, Henry Charles. *History of the Spanish Inquisition*. 4 vols. New York: The Macmillan Company, 1906-07.

_____. *The Inquisition in the Spanish Dependencies*. New York: The Macmillan Company, 1922.
There are several errors, especially where he borrows from secondary sources or relies on others.

Lewin, Boleslao. *Mártires y conquistadores judíos en la America España*. Buenos Aires: Editorial Candelabro, n.d.
There are only four sketches of Mexican Jews. There is no Index and the author indulges in minor flights of fancy.

Library of Congress. *Handbook of Manuscripts*. Washington: U.S. Government Printing Office, 1918.

Libro primero de votos de la inquisición de México (1573-1600). Mexico: Imprenta Universitaria, 1949.

Los judios en la Nueva España. Introduction by Alfonso Toro. Publicaciones AGN. Vol. XX. México: Talleres de Gráficos de la Nacion, 1932.
There is no Index. Much of the material concerns non-Jews.

Martinez del Rio, Pablo. *Alumbrado*. México: Porrúa Hermanos, 1937.

Mayer, William. *Early Travelers in Mexico, 1534-1816*. México, D.F.: Privately printed, 1961.

Mecham, J. Lloyd. *Church and State*. Chapel Hill: University of North Carolina Press, 1934.

Medina, José Toribio. *Historia del Tribunal del Santo Oficio de la Inquisición en México ampliada por Julio Jiménez Rueda*. México, D.F.: Ediciones Fuente Cultural, 1952.
This edition makes obsolete the 1905 edition.

Mendez Plancarte, Alfonso. *Poetas novohispanos*. México: Ediciones de la Universidad Nacional Autónoma de México, 1942.

Menendez y Pelayo, Marcelino. *Historia de los heterodoxos españoles*. 8 vols. Buenos Aires: n.d.

Millares Carlo, Agustin. *Reportorio bibliográfico de los archivos mexicanos y los europeos y norteamericanos de interés para la historía México*. Mexico: Universidad Nacional Autónoma de México, 1959.

Monin, José. *Los judíos en la América Española*. Benos Aires: n.n., 1939.

Neuman, Abraham. *The Jews in Spain*. 2 vols. Philadelphia: Jewish Publishing Society, 1942.

Pallares, Eduardo. *El procedimiento inquisitorial*. México: Imprenta Universitaria, 1951.

Prescott, William H. *History of the Conquest of Mexico*. New York: Random House, n.d.

Puigblanch, D. Antonio. *The Inquisition Unmasked*. London: n.n., 1816.

Riva Palacio, Vicente and Payno, Manuel. *El libro rojo*. México: Díaz de León y White Editores, 1870.
    This edition has excellent lithographs by Iruarte.

_____. *México a través de los siglos*. 5 vols. México: Publicaciones Herrerias, n.d.
    Especially Vol. II. Riva Palacio wrote only part and acted as general editor.

Robles, Antonio de. *Diario de sucesos notables*: 1665-1703. México: Editorial Porrúa, 1946.

Roth, Cecil. *A History of the Marranos*. New York: Meridian Books and the Jewish Publication Society of America, 1959.

Soustelle, Jacques. *The Daily Life of an Aztec*. Translated from French. London: Whitfield & Nicholson, 1961.

Teja Zable, Alfonso. *Guide to the History of Mexico*. México: Secretaria de Relaciones Exterior, 1935.

Toro, Alfonso. *La familia Carvajal*. 2 vols. México, D.F.: Editorial Patria, 1944.

Vaillant, George C. *The Aztecs of Mexico*. Great Britain: Penguin Books, 1956.

Villegas, Alfonso de. *Flos Sanctorum: Historia general de la vida y hechos de Jesus Cristo y todos los santos*. Madrid: n.n., 1593.

Wilson, Robert A. *Mexico and Its Religions*. New York: Harper, 1855.

Zimmels, H. J. *Ashkenazim and Sephardim*. London: Oxford University Press, 1958.

The Bibliography is not intended to be exhaustive. It is the skeleton of primary readings and sources for the colonial era of the history of Mexican Jewry. For further study and sources, the reader may consult the bibliographies in the works of Mair José Benardete, Richard E. Greenleaf, Cecil Roth, and Alfonso Toro; and in the *Enciclopedia Judaica Castellana,* Vol. VII, p. 428; and the articles of George Alexander Kohut, Cyrus Adler, and Nuñez y Dominquez, Ernst Schwarz and Rafael Heliodoro Valle listed *infra.* Lack of familiarity with the *Harkness Collection* and the twenty volumes of Mexican Inquisition Documents of the *David Fergusson Collection* in the Library of Congress, Washington, D.C., resulted in their omission in the Bibliography proper.

ARTICLES AND PERIODICALS

Adler, Cyrus. "Trial of Jorge de Almeida by the Inquisition in Mexico," *PAJHS*, IV (1896), 29-79.

Adler, Elkan N., and Abraham Erlanger. "Collections," *PAJHS*, XL, 115.

AGN Boletin. Vols. VI (1935), VII (1936), VIII (1937). A paleographed summary of the proceso de Tomás Treviño de Sobremonte.

Cadenhead, Ivie E., Jr. "The G. R. G. Conway Collection in the Gilcrease Institute: A Checklist," *HAHR*, XXXVIII (August 1958), No. 3.

Carreño, Alberto Maria. "Luis de Carvajal, El Mozo," *Memorias de la Academía de la Historia de México*, XV, No. 1 (January—March 1956), México, D.F.

Conway, G. R. G. "Hernando Alonso, A Jewish Conquistador with Cortés in Mexico," *PAJHS*, XXXI (1928), 9-31.

Estrada y Escobedo, Pedro de. *"Relacion sumaria del auto particular de fe que el tribunal del Santo Oficio . . . a 16 de Abril, 1646."* Printed monograph, México: Francisco Robledo, 1646.

Fergusson, David. "Proceso de Gabriel de Granada," translation into English with a Preface by Cyrus Adler. *PAJHS*, VII (1899), 1-128.

Inquisition Documents, Notes on. *PAHJS*, XIX, 157-161; and XX, 145-151.

Kohut, George Alexander. "Martyrs of the Inquisition in South America," *PAHJS*, IV, 101-187.
    This and the article by Cyrus Adler, *supra*, must be judged by the time in which they were written. There are several inaccuracies. Kohut includes personalities from Mexico.

Lewin, Boleslao. "Los Marranos: Un intento de definición." A monograph printed by *Colegio Libre de Estudios Superiores*, Buenos Aires, 1946.

Liebman, Seymour B. "Hernando Alonso: First Jew on the North American Continent," *Journal of Inter-American Studies*, V, No. 2 (April, 1963).

_____. "The Jews of Colonial Mexico," *HAHR*, XLIII, No. 1 (February 1963). No. 1.

Mallery, Garrick. "Israelite and Indian." Proceedings in *American Association for Advancement of Science*, XXXVIII (Salem, 1890).

Mariscal, Mario. *Resena historica del AGN*, México, Secretaria de Gobernación, 1946.

McClaskey, Josephine Yocum. "Inquisition Papers of Mexico: II. The Trial of Luis De Cruz, 1656," *Research Studies of the State College of Washington*, XV, No. 1 (March 1947).

"Mexican Inquisition," references in *PAJHS*, II, 73; III, 104-147; V, 46, 47; XLI, 107; XLV, 151; XLVI, 12, 101, 105, 326, 480-81, 483; XLVII, 48-52; XLIX, 202-204.

Nunemaker, J. Horace. "Inquisition Papers of Mexico: 1. The Trial of Simon de León, 1647," *Research Studies of the State College of Washington*, XIV, No. 1 (March 1946).
    This and the McClaskey article each contain a paleographed transcript and an English transcript. They are noteworthy contributions.

Nuñez y Dominquez, José de. "Los judíos en la historia y literatura Mexicana," *Judaica*, No. 139 (Buenos Aires, January 1945).

Perira, Mendez. "Jewish Heretics Executed by Inquisition," *PAJHS*, VIII, 9.

Ricard, Robert. "Pour un etude du Judaisme portugais au Mexique pendant la periode colonial," *Revue D'Histoire Moderne* (Paris, August 1939).
    His *Spiritual Conquest of Mexico*, published in French and Spanish, are must reading for colonial Mexico although there is no data regarding Jews.

Rubio Mané, J. Ignacio. "AGN." *Revista de historia de America*, No. 9, (México, August 1940), 63-169.

Schwarz, Ernst. "Sources for the Study of the Jews in America South of the U.S.," *Inter-American Bibliographical Review* (Washington, D.C., 1941-1942), I, 14, 229-237.

Street, J. "The G. R. G. Conway Collection in Cambridge University Library: A Checklist," *HAHR*, XXXVII, 60-181.

Thornton, A. P. "The G. R. G. Conway MSS. Collection in the Library of the University of Aberdeen," *HAHR*, XXXVI, (1956), 345-347.

Valle, Rafael Heliodoro. "Judíos en México," *Revista chilena de historia y geografia* (September-December 1936), LXXXI, No. 89.

Weinfeld, Eduardo. "Los judíos de México," *Judaica*, No. 85 (Buenos Aires, July 1940).

_____. "La figura del judío en la literatura mexicana," *Judaica*, No. 127 (Buenos Aires, January 1944).

NOVELS

Barron, Alexander. *The Golden Princess*. London: n.n., 1959.

Jiménez Rueda, Julio. *Moisen*. Introduction by Antonio Caso. Mexico: n.n., 1924.
This book describes many customs of the Jews during the colonial era. The author held a high position in the *AGN*. His interest in Inquisition documents led him to write about the Mexican Jews. Luis González Obregón and Alfonso Toro, who held similar positions, were similarly inspired. Unfortunately, they knew little about Judaism and its ritual. Consequently there are some errors and misconceptions.

Riva Palacio, Vicente. *Monja y casada, virgen y martir,* 2 vols. Mexico: n.n., 1943.

_____. *Martin Garatuza,* 2 vols. Mexico: n.n., 1945.

Sierra O'Reilly, Justo. *La hija del judío,* 2 vols. Mexico: n.n., 1959.

The last three books were originally published in the nineteenth century. *La hija del judío* ran in serial form for a year and a half in the newspaper in Mérida, Yucatán, 1848-49.

Alphabetical List

Abeña, Manuel de, 1119
Acevedo, Vaez de (also Sebastian Baez de Acevedo), 352, 613, 649
Acosta, Andres de, 249
Acosta, Antonio, 392
Acosta, Cristobal de, 802
Acosta, Enrique Jorge de, 1186
Acosta, Francisco, 282, 326, 523, 819, 820
Acosta, Manuel de, 139
Acosta, Manuel (also known as Francisco de Torres), 330, 333, 392, 405, 491, 499, 507, 523, 524, 527, 721, 1169
Acuna, Alvarode, 441, 502, 504, 505, 530, 532, 711
Adame, Esteban, 329
Agart, Gaspar de, 1118
Aguilar, Francisco Suarez de, 799
Aguilar, María de, 574
Aguilera, Teresa de—y Roche, 863
Agurto, Leonor de, 567
Alarcon, Cristobal de, 245
Alaren, Fray Fernando de, 442
Alba, Isabel de, 639
Albalez, Julian de, 502
Alburquerque, Francisco de, 920
Alcazar, María Felipa, 939
Alexander, Juan Martin de, 125
Alfar, Gaspar de, 483
Alfaro, Bartolome, 575
Alfaro, Gaspar (see Rodriguez, Gaspar Alfaro)
Allon, Juan de (see also Ayllon), 493
Almeida, Jorge de, 51, 58, 145, 983
Almeyda, Andres, 333, 491
Almeyda—see Almeida
Almonacer, Miguel de, 349, 390, 444
Alonso, Hernándo, 133
Alonso, Hernándo, 1039
Altamirano, Fray Lorenzo, 47, 121
Altamirano, P., 294
Alva, Beatriz de, 505
Alva, Manuel, 506
Alvalez, Juan de (see Alvarez)
Alvarado, Diego de (alias Muñoz), 874, 880
Alvarado, Juan de (see Juan García)
Alvarez, Isabel, 1158
Alvares, Jorge, 63, 66, 149, 161, 998
Alvarez, Fernándo—Pliego, 27
Alvarez, Francisco, 1055

Alvarez, Jorge (see Alvares)
Alvarez, Juan de (also Alvalez), 614
Alvarez, Luis—de Acosta, 277, 282
Alvarez, Manuel, 98
Alvarez, Manuel—de Arellano, 404, 524, 734, 1129
Alvarez, D. Mayor, 542
Alvarez, Pelayo, 1061
Alvarez, Pedro, 630
Alvarez, Simon, 525
Alvaro, Rodríguez, 132
Amezquita, Fernando, 806
Amezquita, Francisco de, 282, 1148
Amezquita, Lope, 398, 576
Amezquita, Luis de, 789
Ampoy, Pierres, 1027
Andrada, Diego—Pardo, 24
Andrada, Isabel (same as Isabel de Carvajal), 842
Andrada, Leonor de, 983
Andrade, Fernándo, 539
Andres, Gaspar, 382, 635
Angel, Fray (see Altamirano)
Angel, Gracia Rol, 121
Angelini, Juan, 950
Angelo, Lorenzo, 294
Angola, Juliano, 788
Antonio, Diego, 508
Antonio, Marco, 993, 1062
Antonio, A. Guerrero Marco, 188
Antunez, Clara, 348, 427, 484, 675
Antúnez, Diego, 401, 459, 472, 501, 677, 1115
Antunez, Isabel (also Antunes or Duarte), 415, 494, 505, 524, 749, 778, 797
Antunez, Manuel, 348, 1115
Arana, Martin, 22
Arango, Juan de (see Juan de Araujo)
Aranz, Francisco de, 719
Araujo, Juan de, 502, 1116
Arbaláez (Arboles), Julian, 611
Arellano, Gabriel de, 664, 669
Areval, Francisco de, 576
Arias, Gabriel, 933
Arias, Gabriel, 502, 507
Arias, Leonor, 23
Arias, María, 348, 354
Arias, Pedro—Maldonado, 620, 1212
Arismena, Antonio—Gogorron, 574
Arizmendi, Pedro de, 975

Fernández, Jorge, 101, 112, 161, 172, 188
Fernández, Jorge, 441B
Fernández, Jose Antonio, 960
Fernández, Juan (see Pedro Fernández)
Fernández, Juan, 668
Fernández, Juan—de Leon, 751, 904, 905
Fernández, Pedro—de Castro (alias Juan Fernández de Castro), 414, 432, 496, 502, 504, 508
Fernández, Capt. Luis—Tristan, 228, 383, 493
Fernández, Manuel, 229
Fernández, Miguel—de Fonseca, 441D
Fernández, Rodrigo—Correa (Bachiller), 382, 554, 563, 1130
Fernández, Rodrigo—Salceda, 1171
Fernández, Simon, 398, 405, 459, 493, 499, 502, 506, 686, 811
Fernández, Simon (also known as Pedro López), 318, 1102
Ferriera, Andres, 167
Figueroa, Alvaro, Ignacio de, 907
Figueroa, Diego de (see Diego Juárez de Figueroa)
Figueroa, Domingo de, 217
Figueroa, Isabel, 441B
Figueroa, Juan de, 205
Figueroa, Nuno (alias Nuno Pereira), 348, 441, 506, 507, 523
Figueroa, Nuno Suarez (also known as Nuno Suarez and possibly D. Suarez de Figueroa), 398, 401, 466, 493
Flamenco, Juan, 152
Flores, Diego, 62
Flores, Domingo, 529
Flores, Gonzálo, 462, 1157
Flores, Juan—Ballinas, 868
Flores, Juan (see Diego Duarte)
Fondeville, Francisco de, 311
Fonseca, Antonio de, 97
Fonseca, Francisco de, 575
Fonseca, Gaspar de, 492, 1214, 1251
Fonseca, Hector, 90, 173, 181, 188
Fonseca, Lopez de (see Francisco López de Fonseca)
Fonseca, Simon de, 491
Fonseca, Tomas de—Castellano, 53, 84, 1086
Fonseca, Tomas, 92, 254, 1085
Francis, Isabel de, 722
Francis, María de, 723
Francisco, Manuel, 853
Franco, Francisco—de Morera, 1180
Franco, Juan, 870
Franco, Miguel, 1002
Franco, Pedro, 757
Frayle, Francisco, 441B
Fuentes, Diego (see Diego Duarte, alias)

G

Gabriel (the younger), 822
Gama, Blanca de, 337
García, Alonso—de Rivera, 654
García, Antonio—Cabezuelo, 271
García, Antonio de, 525
García, Francisco, 924
García, Ines, 186
García, Juan (alias Juan de Alvarado), 1223
García, Juan (el Conde), 251
García, Juan—del Brocel, 805
García, Juan (alias de la Soria and de Santa Ana), 289
Gayan Family, 660
Gerónimo, Gaspar, 305
Gil, José—Taboada, 949
Gil, Manuel—de la Guardia, 99, 133, 166, 181
Gil, Rafael—Rodríguez, 961
Gogorron, Palomeno, 975
Gómez, Ana, 318, 331, 401, 492, 633, 1102, 1222
Gómez, Ana—de Chaves, 1147
Gómez, Ana—Portillo, 318
Gómez, Antonia, 520
Gómez, Antonio, 101, 104, 159, 188, 201
Gómez, Antonio—Carballo, 679
Gómez, Bartolome, 398
Gómez, Beatriz, 16
Gómez, Catalina, 402
Gómez, Catalina—La Cartuja, 1182
Gómez, Cristobal, 136, 667
Gómez, Diego, 137
Gómez, Diego—Pereira, 264
Gómez, Duarte, 276
Gómez, Francisco—de Medina, 502
Gómez, Francisco—Texoso, 1120
Gómez, Frutos—Casillas, 197
Gómez, Gabriel, 399
Gómez, Gabriel—Texoso, 502
Gómez, González, 8
Gómez, Gracia, 1183
Gómez, Isabel, 398
Gómez, Juan, 266
Gómez, Juan, 1158
Gómez, Juana, 61
Gómez, Luis—Lobo, 575
Gómez, Manuel—de Acosta, 879
Gómez, Manuel—Navarro, 61
Gómez, Manuel—de Silvera, 1060
Gómez, María, 318, 320, 590, 631, 1005, 1102, 1161
Gómez, María—Navaro, 132
Gómez, Moises, 892
Gómez, Pedro—Texoso, 399
Gómez, Rafael—Cardoso, 678

Gómez, Rafael—Texoso, 337, 407
Gómez, Thome and Tome, 402, 412, 504
González, Andres—de Saavedra, 838, 839
González, Alonso, 193
González, Alvaro, 105
González, Antonio—Xanayea, 382, 636
González, Beatriz, 43
González, Catalina, 525
González, Capt. Diego-Figueredo, 883
González, Francisco, 528
González, Garcia—Bermegero, 29, 1064
González, José, 895
González, Juan, 43
González, Juan, 303
González, Juan—de Escobar, 508
González, Luis, 1184
González, Luisa, 974
González, Magdalena, 525
González, Pedro, 628, 737
González, Rufina, 273
González, Simon, 1052
Goyz, Fernándo—Matos, 502, 603
Granada, Antonio de, 337
Granada, Gabriel de, 204, 405, 410, 452,
    491, 496, 1122, 1125
Granada, Isabel de, 414, 496, 718
Granada, Manuel de, 398, 400, 409, 412,
    491, 493, 501, 502, 507, 1165
Granada, Rafael de, 204, 394, 399, 405,
    453, 491, 496, 1122, 1125
Granados, Fabian, 1050
Guerra, Alonso, 133
Guerrero, A.—Marco Antonio, 188
Guevara, Pedro de, 492
Guillermo, Juan, 920
Gutiérrez, Gaspar, 524
Gutiérrez, Pedro, 894

H

Henero, Pedro, 837
Henriquez (also spelled Enríquez)
Henriquez, Beatriz, 1130
Henriquez, Clara, 337
Henriquez, Justa, 335
Henriquez, María, 335, 337
Henriquez, Vicente (alias Francis Home;
    see Home)
Heredia, Anton de, 20
Hernán Simón—de Torres, 400
Hernández, Beatriz, 4
Hernández, Beatriz, 335
Hernández, Diego—Victoria, 108, 109,
    134, 137, 142, 143, 166, 169
Hernández, Domingo, 318
Hernández, Enríquez, 402
Hernández, Felipe, 759

Hernández, Francisco, 75
Hernández, García, 3
Hernández, Gaspar, 875
Hernández, Isabel Clara, 75
Hernández, Jorge, 26
Hernández, Manuel, 137
Hernández, Miguel, 91
Hernández, Pedro, 69
Hernández, Pedro—de Alvor, 13
Hernández, Pedro—de Castro, 414
Hernández, Sebastian, 166
Herrador, Diego, 39
Herrera, Agustin—Campos, 417
Herrera, Antonio, 295, 641
Herrera, Cristobal de, 227, 773
Herrera, Francisco de, 640
Herrera, Francisco de—Campos, 417
Herrera, Luis de, 823, 884
Herrero, Hernando, 1039
Herrero, Xines de—Osto, 743
Holgado, Alonso, 930
Home, Francisco (alias Vicente Enríquez
    and Violante Enríquez), 335, 372, 412,
    437
Huerta, Antonio de, 329
Huerta, Isabel de la (see also Enríquez,
    Isabel), 348, 402, 491
Huerta, Miguel de, 1122
Hurtado, Fray Francisco, 213

I

Ibernia, Juan de, 836
Ignacio, Fr. Jospe de San, 904, 905 (see
    also Ignacio, Joseph)
Ignacio, Joseph, 751, 904, 905
Irearte, Bernardo, 829
Isabel, 364, 832

J

Jabeira, Antonio, 441B
Jacinto, Jorge—Bazan, 338, 342, 343, 344,
    814, 855, 1137, 1208, 1244
Javares, Manuel (Toro identifies as
    Suarez), 110
Jeera, fulano, 827
Jerónima, Esperanza, 412, 414, 501
Jiménez, José, 817
Jimenez, Juan—Piquero, 274
Jorge, Domingo, 898, 1032
Jorge, Francisco (tuerto), 136
Jorge, Francisco, 401
Jorge, Pedro, 182
Jorge, Pedro, 569
Juan (mulato), 652

Juan (negro), 1036
Juana (wife of Simon Baez), 333
Juárez, Antonio, 402
Juárez, Blanca, 855, 1137, 1207
Juárez, Diego—de Figueroa, 406, 428, 1209, 1247
Juárez, Gaspar, 339, 393, 405, 1135, 1137
Juárez, Manuel, 1105
Juárez, Melchor, 519, 1070
Juárez, Simon Espinosa, 1109, 1132

L

Langourán, Juan, 1176
Laponte, Justa, 499
Laureano, Juan—de Burgos, 946
Legan, Pedro, 835
Leon, Ana de—Carvajal, 1159
Leon, Catalina de, 131, 1066
Leon, Catalina de, 1067
Leon, Fr. Cristobal de, 869
Leon, Diego de, 262
Leon, Duarte de—Xaramillo, 318, 588, 593, 594, 596, 699, 784, 1127, 1221, 1232, 1235
Leon, Enrique de, 803
Leon, Francisco de, 1200
Leon, Francisco Marques de, 309, 596
Leon, Francisco de—Xaramillo, 1127
Leon, Gonzálo de, 29A
Leon, Jorge de (see also Jorge Duarte), 601
Leon, José del, 896
Leon, Juan Antonio de—Guzman, 903
Leon, Juan Fernández de, 904, 905
Leon, Juana de, 333
Leon, Lope de—Mendoza Alencastro, 886, 896, 897
Leon Manuel de, 871, 889, 1175
Leon, María de, 300, 398, 816
Leon, María C., 441
Leon, Pedro de, 525
Leon, Pedro—de Ayala, 48
Leon, Ponce de, see Figueroa, Alvarez Ignacio de
Leon, Simon de, 594, 1221
Lescano, Fernándo, 876
Lima, Pedro de, 286
Linares, Capt. Domingo de, 514
Lombardo, Don Guillen—de Guzman, 350
López, Alonso, 285
López, Alvaro—Mesa, 327
López, Ana, 78, 147, 188
López, Ana—de Chavez, 1158
López, Antonio, 990
López, Antonio, 991
López, Antonio—Blandon, 318, 1107
López, Antonio, 183, 188, 293

López, Antonio—de Orduña, 403, 495, 792, 1108
López, Beatriz, 473, 491, 576
López, Bernard—de Mendizabal, 566, 858, 860, 861, 863, 864
López, Blas, 451, 507, 530 (2)
López, Coztanza, 528
López, Diego, 135, 147, 233
López, Diego, 337, 1078, 1225
López, Diego—de Granada, 401
López, Diego—Lucena, 492
López, Diego—Coson (alias Diego López Núñez), 571
López, Diego—Regalon (alias Felipe López, 78, 105, 132
López, Diego—Rivera, 307, 508
López, Duarte, 862, 873
López, Elena (see also Elena de Silva), 457
López, Felipa, 132
López, Felipe (see Diego López de Regalon)
López, Felipe—de Norona, 371, 402, 508, 1122
López, Francisco—de Altavista, 337
López, Francisco—Blandon, 314, 318, 319, 591, 1102, 1145, 1162
López, Francisco (el chato) also known as Francisco López Diaz (el chato— flat nose), 354, 398, 400, 412, 456, 496, 497, 502, 687, 1207
López, Francisco—Correa, 382, 547, 576
López, Francisco—Enríquez, 133, 134, 158, 182
López, Francisco—Enríquez, 412, 493, 503
López, Francisco—de Fonseca (see Francisco Méndez), 337, 433, 434
López, Francisco—Lobo, 546, 574
López, Gonzalo—de Aguardia, 398
López, Ines, 412, 502, 1171
López, Isabel—Cardado, 316, 318, 1106
López, Juan, 761
López, Juan—Bravo, 227
López, Juan—Enríquez, 502
López, Juan—de la Guarda, 502
López, Juan—Mejia, 928
López, Juana—Christianos, 392
López, Luis—de Huerta, 412
López, Mateo, 826
López, Mayor, 1162
López, Manuel, 192
López, Manuel, 570, 1167
López, Manuel—Nunez, 391, 412
López, Miguel—Correa, 565
López, P. Home, 337, 366
López, Pedro, 1102, 1104
López, Pedro, 236

Rios—see Rodríguez
Rios, Gabriel, 1042
Rios, Pedro, 1053
Riosas, Pedro, 1082
Riupo, 170
Rivera Family, 519
Rivera, Alonso de, 193
Rivera, Ana, 399
Rivera, Antonia de, 332
Rivera, Beatriz de (also known as
  Beatriz Morales), 133
Rivera, Blanca de (alias Blanca Méndez),
  333, 337, 351, 353, 365, 377, 378, 381,
  390, 401, 411, 414, 415, 476, 496, 500,
  505, 508, 524, 577, 728, 798, 1019,
  1021, 1122, 1199
Rivera, Catalina—Maldonado, 337
Rivera, Catalina de, 365, 379, 404, 419,
  458, 500, 501, 502, 524, 580
Rivera, Clara de, 365, 398, 402, 404, 405,
  406, 412, 415, 441A, 482, 491, 497,
  499, 505, 524, 676, 729, 777, 1122
Rivera, Guiomar de, 1197
Rivera, Isabel de, 349, 363, 365, 376, 377,
  378, 390, 398, 406, 414, 415, 487, 495,
  496, 497, 502, 503, 513, 720, 1122
Rivera, Margarita de, 297, 356, 404, 569,
  703, 1122
Rivera, Maria de, 297, 348, 365, 390, 397,
  398, 399, 402, 403, 409, 412, 453, 491,
  496, 497, 499, 500, 502, 503, 505, 506,
  524, 573, 576, 717, 788, 793, 1165
Rivero, Juan (ironworker), 611, 655
Robles, Antonio de, 790
Robles, Gaspar de, 333, 335, 402, 412,
  507, 508, 519, 692, 787
Rodríguez, Alvaro—Achocado, 106
Rodríguez, Ana, 337, 412
Rodríguez, Ana—de Matos, 1255
Rodríguez, Andre (& Andres), 77, 146,
  1043, 1074
Rodríguez, Antonio—Arias, 414, 447, 504,
  573, 605, 622, 1134
Rodríguez, Antonio, 1047, 1100
Rodríguez, Antonio—Carrasco, 165
Rodríguez, Antonio—Núñez, 337, 502, 680
Rodríguez, Baltazar, 46
Rodríguez, Baltazar de Carbajal Rodríguez
  (also known as Baltazar de Andrada),
  984
Rodríguez, Beatriz, 335, 409, 772
Rodríguez, Beatriz—Alva, 530
Rodríguez, Blanca, 412, 492, 791
Rodríguez, Catalina, 181
Rodríguez, Costanza, 74, 181, 183, 185,
  188, 1099
Rodríguez, Cristobal—Méndez, 524

Rodríguez, Diego, 1172
Rodríguez, Diego—Arias, 338, 605, 606,
  608, 775, 1134
Rodríguez, Diego—García, 938
Rodríguez, Domingo, 1049, 1100
Rodríguez, Domingo (alias Domingo Díaz)
  1099, 1204
Rodríguez, Domingo, 335
Rodríguez, Domingo, 1031, 1071
Rodríguez, Duarte, 87, 101, 133, 188
Rodríguez, Duarte—Tejoso, 348, 399, 502,
  567, 708, 1133, 1233
Rodríguez, Enrique—Obregon, 1199
Rodríguez, Esperanza, 337
Rodríguez, Esperanza, 421, 426, 491, 495,
  507, 508, 533, 582, 607, 1110
Rodríguez, Family, 51
Rodríguez, Fernándo, 450, 553, 1130
Rodríguez, Francisca Núñez (alias Rios),
  1154
Rodríguez, Francisco, 136, 156, 157
Rodríguez, Francisco, 561, 665
Rodríguez, Francisco, 203
Rodríguez, Francisco, 284, 305
Rodríguez, Francisco, 1091
Rodríguez, Francisco, 1092
Rodríguez, Francisco—Carrasco, 415
Rodríguez, Francisco—Carvallo, 194,
  224, 231
Rodríguez, Francisco (alias Francisco
  Rodríguez de Cea), 100, 102
Rodríguez, Francisco—Desa, 79, 89, 1088
Rodríguez, Francisco—de Ledezma, 996,
  1092
Rodríguez, Francisco—Matos, 52, 842,
  980, 982, 984, 992, 1042, 1052, 1073,
  1159
Rodríguez, Francisco—de Molina (alias
  Francisco Machado), 176, 187
Rodríguez, Francisco (alias Francisco
  Núñez), 83, 89, 131
Rodríguez, Gabriel, 384
Rodríguez, Gaspar—Alfaro, 348, 389,
  390, 402, 525
Rodríguez, Gaspar, 232
Rodríguez, Gaspar (also known as Gaspar
  Rodríguez de Segura), 491, 502, 505,
  576
Rodríguez, Gerónimo, 670
Rodríguez, Guimor (also known as Gui-
  mor Núñez), 337 (2)
Rodríguez, Gonzálo, 536
Rodríguez, Hernán—de Herrera, 1061
Rodríguez, Hernándo, 382
Rodríguez, Hernándo—de Herrera, 54,
  57, 131